To Colin Gibson
from
Mary Balfour
Jan 3. 1974.

COOKING AND CATERING
THE WHOLEFOOD WAY

Cooking and Catering the Wholefood Way

Ursula M. Cavanagh

Foreword by
Yehudi Menuhin

London
FABER AND FABER

First published in 1970
by Faber and Faber Limited
24 Russell Square London WC1
Printed in Great Britain by
Latimer Trend & Co Ltd Plymouth

ISBN 0 571 09283 7

CONTENTS

Foreword by Yehudi Menuhin   *page* 7

Introduction   9

*Miscellaneous Information and Hints, Oven
Temperatures, Quantities, Measures, etc.*   11

1. BREAKFAST DISHES   17

2. LUNCHEON DISHES   23

3. VEGETABLES   43

4. SWEET DISHES   51

5. SUPPER DISHES   71

6. SOUPS   85

7. SALADS AND SANDWICH FILLINGS   91

8. HERBS AND SPICES   101

9. BREAD—SCONES—CAKES—BISCUITS   107

Specimen Menus for Three Weeks   127

Wholefood Suppliers   134

Index   137

5

FOREWORD

Perhaps of all books relevant to education and the community this book is the most important to appear!

When children are already being born drug addicts and condemned to cancer in infancy, no doubt the heralds of millions such to come, give me any day a simple earthenware bowl of wholesome stoneground wholemeal porridge or any of the other honest to goodness recipes in this book. I will sacrifice every dolled up and mummified food, artificial flavouring, artificial colour, artificial preservatives, insecticides, chemical fertilizers, together with all the equally phoney words of almost every political or ecclesiastical speech or sermon in recorded history. I would even sacrifice a great many of our voluminous reports, researches, surveys, and statistics, so often, if not outrightly misleading merely repeating the already obvious.

I would certainly keep a few of Churchill's speeches, nor would I give up one line of Shakespeare, one note of Beethoven, one violin of Stradivarius or any other portion of our irreplaceable heritage in art and literature.

By the same token I would not sacrifice one vital cell in any of our children's bodies, be he white, black, yellow or red, which vital life is precisely what our civilization is hell bent on destroying.

That is why this book for schools, homes, hospitals, prisons, office and factory canteens and all other institutions—the first of its kind—is a signpost towards what could become a better, more honest, more beautiful and happier world.

Foreword

Whatever merits the Y.M. School may have, one fact is evident, that Mrs. Cavanagh's catering and cooking will always rank as a major contribution, a major example to school and institution food.

These statements are upheld by our record in terms of sickness as in terms of work, study, and general activity and high morale—the proof is in the pudding!

YEHUDI MENUHIN

INTRODUCTION

This is a book of recipes for schools, hospitals, homes, and all institutions where sound nutrition is of paramount importance.

The emphasis is on natural whole foods such as stone-ground wholewheat flour, brown sugar, natural unpolished rice and honey. These together with free-range eggs and, wherever possible, plenty of compost-grown fruit and vegetables are the basic ingredients of wholefood cooking. Where 'commercial' products are used (fish fingers, canned goods etc.), as indeed they often must be when one is catering for numbers, one must clearly purchase the best and purest quality available. Where finances permit, earthenware, pyrex, or steel utensils are preferable to aluminium.

There is a list of dishes at the beginning of each chapter to make menu-planning easier, and specimen menus for three weeks at the end of the book. There is also a list of suggested additions to the store cupboard and information about wholefood suppliers.

The recipes are made out for sixty persons but can be easily adapted to a greater or lesser number.

URSULA M. CAVANAGH
The Yehudi Menuhin School
Stoke D'Abernon
Surrey

Miscellaneous Information and Hints

USEFUL AMOUNTS TO KNOW

    ¼ lb. tea will make approx. 50 cups
    1 pint of milk is required for 50 cups
    ½ lb. sugar for 50 cups
    1 quarten loaf will give 100 thin slices
    ½ lb. butter is required for 50 sandwiches
    ½ lb. sandwich spread for 50 sandwiches
    1 quart of ice cream makes 12 servings

HANDY MEASURES

Wholewheat flour	2 tablespoons	= 1 oz.
Barbados sugar	1 cup	= 8 oz.
Grated cheese	4 tablespoons	= 1 oz.
Wholewheat breadcrumbs (fresh)	1 cup	= 2 oz.
Brown rice	1 cup	= 8 oz.
Syrup	1 tablespoon	= 1 oz.
Semolina	1 cup	= 6 oz.
Rolled oats	1 cup	= 3 oz.
Currants	1 cup	= 5 oz.
Oatmeal	1 cup	= 5 oz.

METRIC WEIGHTS AND MEASURES

Approximate equivalents	*Exact equivalents*
½ oz. = 15 grams (g)	14·2 grams

Miscellaneous Information and Hints

Approximate equivalents		*Exact equivalents*
1 oz.	= 30 grams	28·3 grams
4 oz.	= 120 grams	
8 oz.	= 240 grams	
1 lb.	= 480 grams	453·6 grams
1 gill	= 1·5 decilitre (dl)	
1 pint	= ½ litre (l)	·568 litre
1¾ pints	= 1 litre	·994 litre

Honey as a Sweetener

1 cup of honey to 2 cups of water makes a syrup for preserving fruit and jam.

Lemon Juice in Mustard

A few drops of lemon juice mixed with your mustard keeps it moist.

Wholewheat Breadcrumbs

To make wholewheat breadcrumbs: put slices of stale bread or toast on baking sheets and cook in slow oven until brown and dry, put through the mincing machine and store in tight-lidded tin.

Using Wholewheat Breadcrumbs

Wholewheat breadcrumbs quickly fried in hot butter with a little finely chopped onion make an interesting topping for all kinds of dishes, especially with fried tomatoes or mushrooms or over cauliflower cheese.

Salty Soups or Stocks

Soups or stocks in which ham or bacon bones are boiled will be less salty if a whole peeled potato is added when cooking and removed at the end of cooking time.

Miscellaneous Information and Hints

Shiny Bun Tops

To give yeast buns a shiny top: dissolve a dessertspoon of Barbados sugar in 1 tablespoon of milk, bring to the boil then brush this over each bun top 10 minutes before the end of cooking time.

Egg and Breadcrumbs

For better results when egging and breadcrumbing add a dessertspoonful of milk and a teaspoon of vegetable oil per egg, plus a little salt and pepper.

Fresh Lettuces

To keep lettuce fresh for several days store unwashed in airtight dustbin or large tightly-lidded saucepan.

To revive limp lettuce, remove outer leaves and end of stalk, separate leaves, wash in very cold water, leave in bowl of iced water and sprinkle with lemon juice. A small piece of coal in the water also helps to make the leaves crisp.

Protein

Dried skimmed milk is the cheapest form of improving the protein content of a meal. 2 lb. of dried milk to 1 gallon water gives a milk with twice the protein and calcium content of fresh milk at less than half the cost.

Parsley

Parsley is not only a source of iron, it is also rich in vitamin C and should be used as often and as lavishly as possible.

Homemade Yoghourt

Boil 1 pint of milk, remove from heat and cool to luke-warm. Stir in 1 tablespoonful of plain yoghourt and mix well with wooden spoon. Pour into well-washed yoghourt cups and stand in heavy saucepan in luke-warm water reaching three-quarters of the way up the cup, cover and leave for 2 hours, topping with hot water occasionally to keep temperature at luke-warm. Remove and refrigerate for several hours.

HOMEMADE SALAD CREAM

See recipe on page 100.

PASTRY

The method in the following recipes is one that is particularly suitable for wholewheat flour. It is a cross between short crust and rough puff, can be used for all purposes, and is virtually fool proof. Other methods may also be used but care must be taken to undercook rather than overcook and water should be used sparingly.

SUGGESTED ADDITIONS TO THE STORE CUPBOARD

100 per cent Compost-grown stone ground wholewheat flour
100 per cent Compost-grown stone ground wholewheat self-raising flour

Barbados sugar	Apple cider vinegar
Demerara sugar	Natural sea salt
Natural brown rice	Soya flour
Honey	Soya beans
Vegetable oil	Herbs and spices

MEAT COOKING TIMES

Roasting

BEEF AND LAMB	20 minutes to the lb. and 20 minutes over
VEAL AND PORK	25 minutes to the lb. and 25 minutes over
POULTRY	25 minutes to the lb.

Boiling

BACON, BEEF, HAM AND PORK	25 minutes to the lb. and 25 minutes over
POULTRY	30 minutes to the lb.

OVEN TEMPERATURES

VERY COOL	225–250° F.	(107–121° C.)	or $\frac{1}{4}$–$\frac{1}{2}$	Gas Regulo
COOL	275–300° F.	(135–149° C.)	or 1–2	Gas Regulo
WARM	325° F.	(163° C.)	or 3	Gas Regulo
MODERATE	350° F.	(177° C.)	or 4	Gas Regulo
FAIRLY HOT	375° F.	(190° C.)	or 5	Gas Regulo
FAIRLY HOT	400° F.	(204° C.)	or 6	Gas Regulo
HOT	425° F.	(218° C.)	or 7	Gas Regulo
VERY HOT	450° F.	(232° C.)	or 8	Gas Regulo
VERY HOT	500° F.	(260° C.)	or 9	Gas Regulo

ABBREVIATIONS

1 tbs. = 1 level tablespoon

1 tsp. = 1 level teaspoon

Chapter 1

BREAKFAST DISHES

1. Muesli
2. Porridge
3. Bacon and Egg
4. Bacon and Chipolata
5. Bacon and Sliced Tomatoes
6. Bacon and Baked Beans
7. Bacon and Mushrooms
8. Chipolata Sausages
9. Scrambled Eggs on Toast
10. Tomatoes on Fried Wholewheat Bread
11. Kippers
12. Fish Fingers
13. Fish Cakes
14. Egg Fritters
15. Boiled Eggs

I

Breakfast Dishes

1. Muesli

3 lb. Scotch oats or wholewheat flakes
1 tin evaporated milk (12
oz.)
8 oz. Barbados sugar
4 pints water

4 oranges
4 apples
4 oz. nuts
8 oz. raisins
8 oz. dates

Dissolve sugar in the water, add the evaporated milk and stir
into uncooked oat flakes. Chop fruit in small pieces and mix
all ingredients together in large bowl. Serve one large tablespoonful per person. Muesli may be made the day before use
and left in the refrigerator overnight.

2. Porridge

2 lb. Scotch oats or wholewheat flakes
2 gallons boiling water

Pour oats into boiling water, stir for 5 minutes, turn off the
heat and leave to settle.

3. Bacon and Egg

2½ lb. streaky bacon (rinded and rashered on No. 4)
60 eggs

Lay bacon rashers on tray and grill for approx. 5 minutes. Fry eggs in vegetable oil.

4. Bacon and Chipolata

2½ lb. streaky bacon (rinded and rashered on No. 4)
4 lb. chipolata sausages (16 to the lb.)

Lay bacon on tray and grill for approx. 5 minutes.
Place sausages on greased tray and grill for approx. 7 minutes, turning when necessary.

5. Bacon and Sliced Tomatoes

2½ lb. streaky bacon (rinded and rashered on No. 4)
4 lb. tomatoes (approx. 6 to the lb.)

Slice each tomato into 5 and place on greased tray, season and grill for a few minutes.
Lay bacon on tray and grill for approx. 5 minutes.

6. Bacon and Baked Beans

2½ lb. streaky bacon (rinded and rashered on No. 4)
2 × A10 tins beans in tomato sauce

Place bacon on tray and grill for approx. 5 minutes. Place beans in double boiler and heat for approx. 45 minutes.

7. Bacon and Mushrooms

2½ lb. streaky bacon (rinded and rashered on No. 4)
3 lb. sliced mushrooms

Lay bacon on tray and grill for approx. 5 minutes. Fry mushrooms gently for 10 minutes in vegetable oil.

8. Chipolata Sausages

8 lb. chipolata sausages (16 to the lb.)

Lay sausages on greased tray and grill for approx. 7 minutes, turning when necessary.

9. Scrambled Eggs on Toast

48 eggs	*sea salt and pepper*
3 pints milk	*3 × 2-lb. wholewheat loaves*
1 lb. margarine	*1½ lb. butter*

Break eggs into double boiler, add milk and margarine, salt and pepper and cook for approx. 1 hour. Serve on buttered toast, allowing ½ slice per person.

10. Tomatoes on Fried Wholewheat Bread

10 lb. tomatoes (approx. 6 to the lb.)
3 × 2-lb. wholewheat loaves

Cut tomatoes in half, lay on greased tray, season and grill for 2 or 3 minutes.

Allow half a slice of bread per person and fry in vegetable oil.

11. Kippers

3 × 7 lb. kipper fillets

Place on trays, cover with water and grill for 10 minutes.

12. Fish Fingers

120 fish fingers

Fry in vegetable oil.

13. Fish Cakes

60 fish cakes

Fry in vegetable oil.

14. Egg Fritters

30 beaten eggs   *3 × 2-lb. wholewheat loaves*
2 pints milk

Slice loaves, cut slices in half, dip in egg and milk mixture, fry in vegetable oil.

15. Boiled Eggs

60 eggs

Put basket containing eggs into boiling water for 6 minutes.

SERVE WHOLEWHEAT TOAST, BUTTER AND HONEY after the main course.

Chapter 2

LUNCHEON DISHES

Meat

16. Roast Beef—Yorkshire Pudding—Horseradish Sauce
17. Roast Lamb—Onion Sauce—Mint Sauce
18. Roast Pork—Apple Sauce
19. Boiled Beef—Dumplings
20. Braised Steak
21. Boiled Bacon—Parsley Sauce
22. Stewed Steak
23. Curry and Rice
24. Savoury Meat Roll
25. Grilled Lamb Chops
26. Liver and Bacon
27. Irish Stew
28. Grilled Pork Chops
29. Steak and Kidney Pie
30. Veal and Ham Pie
31. Chicken and Mushroom Pie
32. Chicken Fricassée and Rice
33. Roast Chicken—Savoury Stuffing—Bread Sauce
34. Minced Beef
35. Sausages
36. Cottage Pie

37. Meat Loaf
38. Toad in the Hole
39. Rissoles
40. Chicken Slaw
41. Cold Ham—Corned Beef—Luncheon Meat
42. Roast Turkey—Bread Sauce—Chestnut and Sausage Meat Stuffing
43. Devilled Turkey
44. Sweet and Sour Pork—Fried Rice

Fish

45. Fried Cod Fillets—Hollandaise Sauce
46. Baked Cod—Egg Sauce—Parsley Sauce
47. Kedgeree
48. Fish Pie
49. Fish Slaw
50. Tuna Fish Salad
51. Fish and Bacon Pie

2

Luncheon Dishes

MEAT

16. Roast Beef   Yorkshire Pudding   Horseradish Sauce

    2 × 7-lb. topside or   *4 oz. dripping*
    2 × 8-lb. sirloin

Place meat in pan with melted dripping, roast in oven 450° F. or Reg. 8 for 15 minutes, reduce the heat to 350° F. or Reg. 4 for $2\frac{1}{2}$ hours approx.

YORKSHIRE PUDDING

    $1\frac{1}{2}$ lb. wholewheat flour   *4 oz. dripping*
    2 pints milk and 1 pint water *sea salt*
    8 eggs   *pepper*

Beat seasoned flour, eggs and milk and water in mixer, balloon whisk speed 3, for 12 minutes. Pour into tins containing heated dripping and bake in oven 450° F. or Reg. 8 for 40 minutes.

HORSERADISH SAUCE

    1 lb. grated horseradish   *$\frac{1}{2}$ oz. sea salt*
    6 oz. apple cider vinegar   *pepper*
    1 pint evaporated milk

Mix all ingredients together.

17. Roast Lamb   Mint Sauce   Onion Sauce

4 × 5-lb. leg of lamb, boned and rolled
4 oz. dripping

Put meat in pans with melted dripping, sprinkle meat with
rosemary, roast in oven 450° F. or Reg. 8 for 15 minutes,
reduce heat to 350° F. or Reg. 4 for approx. 2 hours.

MINT SAUCE

8 oz. chopped mint	*4 oz. boiling water*
2 oz. Barbados sugar	*1 pint apple cider vinegar*

Mix mint and sugar, pour on boiling water and add the vinegar.

ONION SAUCE

2 lb. onions	*12 oz. margarine*
4 pints water	*sea salt*
4 pints milk	*pepper*
12 oz. wholewheat flour	

Chop onions and boil in salted water until soft. Bring 3 pints
of milk to the boil in double saucepan, mix flour to a smooth
paste with 1 pint cold milk and add to saucepan, add margarine, pepper, onions and onion water, and cook all together
for a further 5 minutes.

18. Roast Pork   Apple Sauce

3 × 7-lb. leg of pork, boned and rolled
8 oz. dripping

Place meat in pans with melted dripping, rub skin with sea
salt and roast in oven 450° F. or Reg. 8 for 20 minutes, reduce
heat to 400° F. or Reg. 6 and cook for 3½ hours approx.

Luncheon Dishes

APPLE SAUCE

8 lb. cooking apples	*1 pint water*
4 oz. Barbados sugar	

Stew apples slowly, withdraw from heat and add sugar.

19. Boiled Beef Dumplings

3 × 7 lb. salt silverside	*3 lb. carrots*
3 lb. onions	*3 lb. turnips*

Cover meat with water, add chopped vegetables and simmer for 3½ hours. Slice meat and serve covered with vegetables.

DUMPLINGS

2½ lb. self-raising whole-wheat flour	*sea salt*
1½ lb. suet	*pepper*

Mix ingredients to a soft dough with water, form into balls and boil gently in meat liquor for 12 minutes.

20. Braised Steak

16 lb. chuck steak	*12 oz. wholewheat flour*
3 lb. onions	*6 Oxo cubes*
3 lb. carrots	*2 oz. Marmite*
1½ gallons water or stock	

Cut steak into required number of slices, fry on each side for a few minutes in vegetable oil then place in casseroles. Chop vegetables, fry, and add to casseroles. Heat stock, mix flour to a smooth paste with a little cold stock and add to boiling stock, flavour with Marmite, Oxo, salt and pepper and pour over meat and vegetables in casseroles. Cook in oven 400° F. or Reg. 6 for 3 hours.

Luncheon Dishes

21. Boiled Bacon Parsley Sauce

3 × 7-lb. hock, boned and rolled

Cover with water and simmer gently for 3 hours, skin.

PARSLEY SAUCE

6 oz. chopped parsley	*½ lb. margarine*
6 pints milk	*sea salt*
6 oz. wholewheat flour	*pepper*

Bring 5 pints milk to the boil in double saucepan, mix flour to a smooth paste with 1 pint cold milk and add to boiling milk, add margarine, parsley and seasoning, and cook all together for a further 5 minutes.

22. Stewed Steak

16 lb. stewing steak	*12 oz. wholewheat flour*
3 lb. carrots	*bouquet garni*
3 lb. onions	*3 additional bay leaves*
1½ gallons water or stock	*4 oz. parsley*
4 oz. dripping	*4 oz. Marmite*
sea salt	*4 Oxo cubes*
pepper	

Chop up meat and vegetables, fry for a few minutes then place in large saucepan, cover with water or stock, add bouquet garni, bay leaves, Oxo, Marmite, salt and pepper, and simmer gently for 3 hours. Mix flour to a smooth paste with cold stock and add to stew ½ hour before it has finished cooking. Remove bouquet garni and bay leaves, sprinkle with chopped parsley.

23. Curry and Rice

16 lb. stewing steak	*4 oz. dripping*
12 pints water	*3 lb. sliced onions*
12 oz. wholewheat flour	*1 lb. cooking apples*
1 lb. sultanas	*8 oz. curry powder*
sea salt	*2 oz. ground ginger*
pepper	*2 oz. turmeric powder*
5 lb. natural brown rice	*2 oz. paprika*

Chop meat, fry for a few minutes in large saucepan, cover with water and cook gently for 3 hours. Fry sliced onions, sultanas, chopped apples, stir in curry powder, turmeric, ginger and paprika, add to meat $\frac{1}{2}$ hour before it is cooked. Mix flour to a smooth paste with cold water and thicken curry just before it is served.

Cook rice in boiling salted water for 20 minutes.

Curry should be served with mango chutney, dessicated coconut, and sliced tomatoes.

24. Savoury Meat Roll

12 lb. minced beef	PASTRY
4 oz. dripping	*4 lb. wholewheat flour*
2 lb. minced onions	*1$\frac{1}{2}$ lb. lard*
12 oz. wholewheat flour	*1$\frac{1}{2}$ lb. margarine*
4 oz. curry powder	*1 pint water*
4 oz. chopped parsley	*salt*
sea salt	*1 egg*
pepper	
garlic powder	
12 pints stock or water	

Fry mince and onions for a few minutes in large saucepan, cover with water or stock and simmer for 1$\frac{1}{2}$ hours. Drain off liquid, mix flour to a smooth paste with a little cold stock and add to mince, flavour with curry powder, parsley and seasoning, allow to cool. Cut lard into salted flour in mixer using dough hook speed 1, gradually add the water, mix for another 2 minutes and turn out on to floured board. Divide into 8 portions, roll out each one, dot with margarine, fold and roll out again, fill with mince, roll up, seal, brush them all with egg and bake in oven 425° F. or Reg. 7 for 1 hour.

25. Grilled Lamb Chops

60 lamb chops

Place on tray, dot with fat, season and grill for approx. 10 minutes on each side.

26. Liver and Bacon

16 lb. ox liver	*1 lb. seasoned wholewheat*
3 lb. streaky bacon	*flour*

Remove skin, dip in flour, fry gently in vegetable oil or dripping. Grill bacon for 5 minutes. Serve with thick brown gravy.

27. Irish Stew

1½ gallons water	*7 lb. onions*
14 lb. middle neck end chops	*1 oz. sea salt*
1 lb. pearl barley	*½ oz. pepper*
7 lb. potatoes	

Place all ingredients in large saucepan, cover with water and simmer gently for 2 hours.

28. Grilled Pork Chops

60 pork chops

Place on tray, dot with fat, season and grill for 12 minutes each side.

29. Steak and Kidney Pie

$1\frac{1}{2}$ *gallons water*
12 oz. wholewheat flour
16 lb. stewing steak
3 lb. ox kidney
3 lb. onions
1 oz. sea salt
$\frac{1}{2}$ *oz. pepper*

PASTRY
4 lb. plain wholewheat flour
$1\frac{1}{2}$ *lb. lard*
$1\frac{1}{2}$ *lb. margarine*
1 pint water
1 egg

Chop meat and onions, put in large saucepan, cover with water and stew gently for $2\frac{1}{2}$ hours, thicken with wholewheat flour and season. Mix lard into salted flour in electric mixer, using dough hook and speed 1, sprinkle in the water slowly, continue mixing for 2 minutes, then turn out on to floured board. Divide into the required number of portions, roll out each portion, dot with margarine, fold and roll out again. Put meat in dishes, cover with pastry, brush with egg and bake in oven 425° F. or Reg. 7 for 1 hour.

30. Veal and Ham Pie

14 lb. stewing veal
7 lb. hock
12 pints water
12 hard-boiled eggs
4 oz. chopped parsley

PASTRY
4 lb. plain wholewheat flour
$1\frac{1}{2}$ *lb. lard*
$1\frac{1}{2}$ *lb. margarine*
1 pint water
2 oz. sea salt
1 egg

Put meat in large saucepan, cover with water, and simmer gently for $1\frac{1}{2}$ hours. Cut up into small pieces and place in pie dishes. Slice hard-boiled eggs and place on top of meat, sprinkle with parsley and fill up dishes with meat liquor. Mix lard into salted flour in mixer using dough hook and speed 1, add water slowly, mix for a further 2 minutes and turn out on

31

to floured board. Roll out, dot with margarine, fold and roll out again, then cut into the required number of portions. Cover meat with pastry, brush with egg and bake in oven 425° F. or Reg. 7 for 1 hour.

31. Chicken and Mushroom Pie

2 × 4-lb. chickens
3 lb. mushrooms
4 oz. parsley

SAUCE
8 pints milk
12 oz. wholewheat flour
8 oz. margarine
1 oz. sea salt
pepper

PASTRY
8 lb. wholewheat flour
3½ lb. lard
3½ lb. margarine
2 pints water
2 oz. sea salt
1 egg

Cover chickens with water and simmer gently for 2 hours. Remove flesh from bones and chop into small pieces. Slice and gently fry the mushrooms. Bring 7 pints of milk to the boil in double boiler, mix flour to a smooth paste with 1 pint of cold milk and add to saucepan and cook all together for a further 5 minutes. Add margarine, seasoning, chicken pieces, mushrooms and chopped parsley. Cut lard into salted flour using dough hook and speed 1, add water slowly, mix for a further 2 minutes and turn out on to floured board. Roll out, dot with margarine, fold and roll out again. Line tins with pastry, fill with chicken mixture, cover with pastry, brush with egg and bake in oven 425° F. or Reg. 7 for one hour.

32. Chicken Fricassée and Rice

4 × 4-lb. chickens
5 lb. natural brown rice

4 oz. chopped parsley

SAUCE

4 pints chicken stock	*1 lb. margarine*
8 pints milk	*1 oz. sea salt*
16 oz. wholewheat flour	*pepper*

Cover chickens with water and simmer gently for 2 hours. Remove meat from bones and chop into small pieces. Bring 7 pints milk to the boil in double boiler, mix flour to a smooth paste with cold milk and add to saucepan. Cook all together for a further 5 minutes. Add stock, seasonings, margarine, parsley, and chicken pieces to sauce. Cook rice in boiling salted water for 20 minutes.

33. Roast Chicken   Bread Sauce   Savoury Stuffing

8 × 3-lb. chickens   *8 oz. dripping*

Place chickens in pans with dripping and roast in oven 450° F. or Reg. 8 for 15 minutes, reduce heat to 350° F. or Reg. 4 and cook for $1\frac{1}{2}$ hours. Serve with bread sauce, savoury stuffing, bacon rolls and chipolatas.

BREAD SAUCE

6 pints milk	*2 onions pricked with cloves*
8 oz. margarine	*sea salt*
$1\frac{3}{4}$ lb. wholewheat bread-crumbs	*pepper*

Heat milk, margarine, breadcrumbs and onions in double boiler, season well. Leave to settle and remove onions before serving.

SAVOURY STUFFING

$2\frac{1}{2}$ lb. wholewheat bread-crumbs	*pepper*
$\frac{3}{4}$ lb. suet	*2 oz. chopped parlsey*
1 oz. mixed herbs	*rind and juice 2 lemons*
salt	*2 eggs*

C   33

Mix dry ingredients, moisten with lemon juice and eggs, bake in greased tins covered with paper in oven 350° F. or Reg 4 for ¾ hour.

34. Minced Beef

16 lb. minced beef	*1 tbs. Marmite*
1½ gallons water or stock	*4 Oxo cubes*
3 lb. chopped onions	*salt*
4 oz. chopped parsley	*pepper*
8 oz. wholewheat flour	*garlic salt*

Fry onions and mince in large saucepan, cover with water and simmer for 2 hours. Remove some of the liquid, mix flour to a smooth paste with cold stock and add to the mince, season with salt, pepper, Marmite, Oxo and garlic salt. Serve with plenty of chopped parsley.

35. Sausages

8 lb. pork or beef sausages (8 to lb.)
4 oz. dripping

Lay on well-greased trays, season and grill for 15 minutes, turning when necessary. Serve with mashed potatoes and thick brown gravy.

36. Cottage Pie

14 lb. minced beef	*sea salt*
12 pints water	*pepper*
2 lb. onions	*garlic salt*
8 oz. wholewheat flour	*14 lb. potatoes*
1 tbs. Marmite	*1 lb. margarine*
4 Oxo cubes	*2 pints milk*
4 oz. parsley	

Fry onions and mince in large saucepan, cover with water and cook for approx. 2 hours, drain off the liquid. Mix flour to a smooth paste with cold water and add to mince, season well and flavour with Marmite, Oxo and parsley. Place in dishes and cover with mashed potatoes, brush with oil and bake in oven 450° F. or Reg. 8 for 45 minutes.

37. Meat Loaf

18 lb. cooked minced beef or	*6 eggs*
leftovers	*garlic salt*
2 lb. minced onions	*salt*
3 lb. mashed potatoes	*pepper*
4 oz. chopped parsley	

Mix all ingredients together, season well, place in greased loaf tins and bake in oven 375° F. or Reg. 5 for 1½ hours. Serve cold with sliced tomatoes.

38. Toad in the Hole

8 lb. pork sausages	BATTER
(8 to lb.)	*2 pints milk*
8 oz. dripping	*2 pints water*
	3 lb. wholewheat flour
	12 eggs
	salt
	pepper

Put seasoned flour, milk, water, and eggs in mixer and beat for 12 minutes, balloon whisk, speed 3. Pour batter into tins containing hot dripping, place sausages in batter and bake in oven 450° F. or Reg. 8 for 1 hour.

39. Rissoles

10 lb. cooked minced beef or leftovers
2 lb. minced onions
salt
pepper
garlic salt

4 oz chopped parsley
2 lb. mashed potatoes
8 eggs
2 lb. wholewheat bread-crumbs

Mix beef, onions, potatoes, parsley and seasoning, form into balls. Dip in egg and breadcrumbs, fry in deep vegetable oil, drain well and serve with sliced tomatoes.

40. Chicken Slaw

2 × 4-lb. chickens
1 lb. raisins
8 lb. dutch cabbage
4 lb. carrots
6 apples

6 oranges
2 pints salad cream
sea salt
pepper
garlic salt

Cover chickens with water and simmer gently for 2 hours. Remove meat from bone and cut into small pieces. Shred cabbage and carrots, cut apples and oranges into small pieces, mix all ingredients together in a large bowl, add salad cream and season well.

41. Cold Ham   Luncheon Meat   Corned Beef

3 × 7-lb. hock
2 × 6 lb. luncheon meat

2 × 6 lb. corned beef

To cook hock cover with water and simmer gently for 3 hours. Skin whilst still hot and sprinkle with breadcrumbs.

42. Roast Turkey   Bread Sauce   Chestnut and Sausage Meat Stuffing

2 × 16-lb. turkeys	*2 lemons*
16 oz. dripping	*4 oz. honey*
4 oz. sea salt	

Rub turkey with salt, lemon juice and honey, put in pan with melted dripping and roast for 20 minutes in oven 450° F. or Reg. 8, then for another 5½ hours approx. in oven 350° F. or Reg. 4. Serve with bread sauce and chestnut and sausage meat stuffing. Cooked ham, chipolata sausages, bacon rolls, and cranberry sauce can all be served with roast turkey.

CHESTNUT AND SAUSAGE MEAT STUFFING

3 lb. chestnuts	*1 lb. wholewheat bread-*
2 lb. sausage meat	*crumbs*
4 lb. butter	*4 eggs*
	6 oz. chopped parsley

Make a small slit in each chestnut, plunge into boiling water and cook for 20 minutes, remove skin. Mash the chestnuts and mix with sausage meat, butter, breadcrumbs, and parsley, bind with eggs, season well, spread in greased trays and bake in oven 350° F. or Reg. 4 for ¾ hour.

BREAD SAUCE

6 pints milk	*2 onions pricked with cloves*
8 oz. margarine	*1 oz. sea salt*
1 lb. 12 oz. wholewheat	*pepper*
breadcrumbs	

Heat milk, margarine, breadcrumbs and onions in double saucepan, season well, leave to settle and remove onions before serving.

Luncheon Dishes

43. Devilled Turkey (PARTY DISH)

2 × 16-lb. turkeys
6 green peppers
1 bottle dry white wine
4 pints single cream
8 oz. wholewheat flour
2 oz. sea salt
pepper

garlic salt
8 lb. brown rice
3 lb. mushrooms
6 pints chicken stock
8 oz. butter
4 bottles Escoffier Sauce
Diable (5¾ oz. size)

Roast turkeys in slow oven for 5½ hours approx. Remove meat from bone and cut into small pieces. Slice and fry mushrooms and peppers in butter in large heavy saucepan, add sauce diable, white wine and stock. Mix flour to a smooth paste with cold stock and add to saucepan, simmer for 5 minutes stirring all the time. Transfer sauce to double saucepan and stir in the turkey pieces. Keep warm and add cream ½ hour before serving. Cook rice in boiling salted water for 20 minutes.

44. Sweet and Sour Pork   Fried Rice

16 lb. best belly of pork
(skinned and cubed)
12 oz. wholewheat flour
2 bottles soya sauce (5½ oz.
size)
8 oz. Barbados sugar
2 pints sweet vinegar
pickles
1 gallon water or stock

BATTER
2 lb. wholewheat flour
12 eggs
2 pints milk
1 pint water
1 oz. sea salt
pepper

Beat flour, eggs, milk and water in mixer with balloon whisk speed 3 for 12 minutes. Boil water, sugar and soya sauce together, add pickles, and thicken sauce by mixing flour to a smooth paste with a little cold water or stock and adding to sauce. Dip pork cubes in batter and fry in vegetable oil for

38

several minutes, then either stir pork cubes into sauce or serve separately with fried rice.

FRIED RICE

5 lb. natural brown rice

Cook in boiling salted water for 20 minutes, then fry in vegetable oil until rice turns colour.

FISH

45. Fried Cod Fillets   Hollandaise Sauce

2 × 7-lb. cod fillet   *3 lb. wholewheat bread-*
8 eggs   *crumbs*

Skin fillets, cut into the required number of portions, dip in egg and breadcrumbs and deep fry in vegetable oil. Serve with lemon slices and hollandaise sauce.

HOLLANDAISE SAUCE

6 pints milk   *8 oz. margarine*
6 oz. wholewheat flour   *1½ pints salad cream*
                                        sea salt, pepper

Bring 5 pints of milk to the boil in double saucepan, mix flour to a smooth paste with 1 pint cold milk and add to saucepan, add margarine, salt, pepper and cook all together for a further 5 minutes. Add salad cream.

46. Baked Cod   Egg Sauce   Parsley Sauce

2 × 7-lb. cod fillets   *sea salt*
8 oz. margarine   *pepper*

Skin fillets, cut into required number of portions, place on trays, dot with margarine, salt and pepper and bake in oven 350° F. or Reg. 4 for ¾ hour. Serve with egg or parsley sauce.

Luncheon Dishes

EGG SAUCE PARSLEY SAUCE

12 chopped hard-boiled eggs	*6 pints milk*
or	*6 oz. wholewheat flour*
8 oz. chopped parsley	*8 oz. margarine*
	sea salt, pepper

Bring 5 pints of milk to the boil in double saucepan, mix flour to a smooth paste with 1 pint of cold milk and add to saucepan, add margarine, salt, pepper and cook all together for a further 5 minutes. Add either chopped hard-boiled eggs or chopped parsley.

47. Kedgeree

2 × 7-lb. smoked cod fillets	*8 oz. chopped parsley*
1 lb. margarine	*4 lb. natural brown rice*
18 chopped hard-boiled eggs	

Cover fish with water and simmer gently for ½ hour. Cook rice in boiling salted water for 20 minutes. Debone fish and cut up into small pieces, add to the rice. Melt margarine and pour over fish and rice, sprinkle with chopped eggs and parsley.

48. Fish Pie

2 × 7-lb. cod fillets	*6 oz. wholewheat flour*
18 eggs	*8 oz. margarine*
8 oz. chopped parsley	*sea salt*
18 lb. potatoes	*pepper*
6 pints milk	

Cover fish with water and simmer gently for ½ hour, debone. Bring 5 pints milk to the boil in double saucepan, mix flour to a smooth paste with 1 pint cold milk and add to the saucepan, add margarine, salt, pepper and cook all together for a further 5 minutes. Add eggs and parsley. Stir fish into sauce, place in pie dishes and cover with mashed potatoes, brush with oil and bake in oven 400° F. or Reg. 6 for 1 hour.

49. Fish Slaw

2 × 7-lb. cod fillets	*garlic salt*
4 lb. carrots	*8 lb. dutch cabbage*
1 lb. raisins	*6 apples*
sea salt	*6 oranges*
pepper	*2 pints salad cream*

Cover fish with water and simmer gently for $\frac{1}{2}$ hour, cool and debone. Shred carrots and cabbage finely, cut oranges and apples into small pieces. Mix vegetables, fruit, fish and raisins together, season well and stir in the salad cream.

50. Tuna Fish Salad

12 × 8-oz. tins tuna fish	*24 eggs*
2 pints salad cream	*8 oz. chopped parsley*
4 lb. natural brown rice	*sea salt, pepper*

Cook rice in boiling salted water for 20 minutes, drain and cool. Add fish, chopped hard-boiled eggs and parsley, season well and stir in the salad cream.

51. Fish and Bacon Pie

2 × 7-lb. cod fillets	*6 pints milk*
2 lb. grated Cheddar cheese	*6 oz. wholewheat flour*
8 oz. margarine	*sea salt, pepper*
3 lb. streaky bacon	*4 oz. chopped parsley*

Bring 5 pints milk to the boil in double saucepan, mix flour to a smooth paste with 1 pint cold milk and add to saucepan, add margarine, salt, pepper and cook all together for a further 5 minutes. Add cheese. Skin fish, cut into required number of portions, place on tray, dot with margarine and bake in oven 350° F. or Reg. 4 for ¾ hour. Grill bacon for 5 minutes approx. Place cooked fish in dishes, top each piece with a rasher of bacon cover with cheese sauce, sprinkle with parsley and serve.

Chapter 3

VEGETABLES

Beetroot	16 lb.
Broad Beans	24 lb.
Brussels Sprouts	20 lb.
Dutch Cabbage	14 lb.
Red Cabbage	14 lb.
Green Cabbage	20 lb.
Cauliflower	30 lb.
Carrots	18 lb.
Celery	20 lb.
Runner Beans	18 lb.
Leeks	18 lb.
Marrow	25 lb.
Onions	16 lb.
Peas	30 lb. fresh 10 lb. frozen
Parsnips	25 lb.
Potatoes (according to method)	14 lb.–20 lb.
Spinach	25 lb.
Swedes	20 lb.
Turnips	20 lb.
Peppers	6 (for slicing in mixed salad)

Vegetables

Tomatoes	8 lb.
Watercress	4 lb.
Lettuce	10
Radishes	15 bundles
Cucumbers	3
Soya Beans	3 lb.

3

Vegetables

Beetroot

Wash, cover with cold water and boil gently for approx. 2 hours or until tender. Skin, slice and sprinkle with parsley. Beetroot may also be eaten raw, chopped into small cubes and mixed with a dressing of two parts of vegetable oil to one of apple cider vinegar.

Broad Beans

Pod beans and put into boiling salted water, the minimum possible, and boil for 20 minutes. When the beans are young the pods should be chopped up and cooked with the beans.

Brussels Sprouts

Remove outer leaves, cut stalks, and wash well. Put into boiling salted water and cook for 15 minutes.

Dutch Cabbage

Remove outer leaves, shred and wash well. It may be dealt with in three different ways:

1. Cooked in a minimum amount of boiling salted water for 15 minutes.
2. Cooked for 5 minutes in one cup of vegetable oil in a tight-lidded saucepan and for a further 5 minutes with the addition of a cup of stock or bouillon.
3. Eaten raw with a dressing of two parts of vegetable oil to one of cider vinegar.

Red Cabbage

Shred and wash well removing all hard stalks. Fry 6 onions and
6 sliced apples in 8 oz. butter or margarine, add 4 oz. apple
cider vinegar, salt, pepper and a few cloves. Add cabbage,
cover and stew gently for 2 hours, adding one cup of stock if
necessary.

Green Cabbage

Remove outer leaves, shred and wash well. Cook in minimum
amount of boiling salted water for 15 minutes or else cook in
1 cup of vegetable oil in tight-lidded saucepan for 5 minutes
and for a further 5 minutes with the addition of 1 cup of
stock or bouillon.

Cauliflower

Remove outer leaves only, break flower into small pieces,
chop green leaves and cook in minimum amount of boiling
salted water for 15 minutes. Cauliflower may also be cooked
in 1 cup of vegetable oil in fast-lidded saucepan for 5 minutes
and for a further 5 minutes with the addition of 1 cup of
bouillon.

Carrots

Wash well and scrape or place in potato machine for a few
minutes. Slice and put into cold water, bring to the boil and
cook for 30 minutes.

Carrots may also be sliced and put into a tight-lidded
saucepan with 1 cup of vegetable oil and cooked for 10 minutes
and for a further 10 minutes with the addition of 1 cup of
bouillon or stock. Serve sprinkled with chopped parsley.

Celery

Separate heads of celery, wash well, and chop into small

pieces. Put in boiling salted water and cook for 15 minutes. Celery may also be cooked in a tight-lidded saucepan in 1 cup of vegetable oil for 5 minutes and for a further 5 minutes with the addition of 1 cup of bouillon or stock.

It is of course delicious raw, or with a dressing of two parts vegetable oil to one part of cider vinegar and a sprinkle of garlic salt and parsley.

Runner Beans

Shred in bean slicing machine and cook in a minimum amount of boiling salted water for 15 minutes.

Leeks

Wash well, remove outer leaves, slice the remaining leaves and cook in boiling salted water for 15 minutes.

Marrow

Peel, cut into small wedges and cook in boiling salted water for 15 minutes. Serve well drained sprinkled with parsley.

Onions

Remove outer leaves and cook in boiling salted water. Onions can also be braised in the oven. Put them in a little vegetable oil seasoned with salt and pepper, cook for about 2 hours.

Peas

Pod and place in boiling salted water, minimum possible, flavoured with two or three twigs of mint, and cook for 15 minutes.

Vegetables

Parsnips

Wash, chop up and place in cold water, bring to the boil and cook for 40 minutes. Parsnips may also be roasted in the oven and take approx. 1½ hours.

Potatoes

OLD POTATOES should be placed in cold water and boiled for approx. 1 hour, preferably unpeeled. (14 lb.)

For frying potatoes (18 lb.) chip and cook in hot vegetable oil.

For roasting (18 lb.) cook first in water for 15 minutes, then in vegetable oil in a very hot oven for approx. 1 hour.

For baking (16 lb.) wash well and place potatoes in hot oven for 2 hours.

NEW POTATOES. Place in boiling salted water with sprigs of mint and boil for 30 minutes.

Spinach

Wash well and place spinach in tight-lidded saucepan with 2 cups of stock or water and cook for 10 minutes.

Swedes

Peel, chop, and place in cold water, bring to the boil and cook for 1 hour approx. Mash in mixing machine with 1 lb. margarine, salt and pepper.

Turnips

Peel, chop, place in cold water and simmer for 1½ hours.

Peppers

Peppers should be washed and the seeds and inside skin removed. They can be shredded or chopped finely and used raw for salads, or fried or baked.

Tomatoes

Wash well, chop or slice and eat raw, sprinkled with parsley.

Watercress

Wash well and serve with a dressing of two parts vegetable oil to one of cider vinegar.

Lettuce

Wash well and use in mixed salads or on its own with a dressing of two parts of vegetable oil to one of cider vinegar, salt, pepper and a little garlic salt.

Radishes

Wash well and eat whole or slice and use for decorating mixed salads.

Cucumbers

Wash well and slice with skin on. Can be eaten with a dressing of two parts of vegetable oil to one of cider vinegar, or used in mixed salads.

Soya Beans

Soak overnight, then simmer gently in same water for 2 hours. Serve hot with butter and sprinkled with parsley or in tomato sauce. They may also be served cold in salads or with a dressing of two parts vegetable oil to one of cider vinegar.

Chapter 4

SWEET DISHES

52. Apple Fritters
53. Pineapple Fritters
54. Banana Fritters
55. Apple Pie
56. Apricot Pie
57. Gooseberry Pie
58. Apple Tart
59. Blackberry and Apple Tart
60. Apricot Tart
61. Gooseberry Tart
62. Rhubarb Tart
63. Apple Crunch
64. Apricot Crunch
65. Pineapple Crunch
66. Rhubarb Crunch
67. Gooseberry Crunch
68. Plum Crunch
69. Apple Sponge
70. Apricot Sponge
71. Apple Meringue
72. Apricot Meringue
73. Pineapple Meringue
74. Baked Apples
75. Stewed Apples
76. Apricot Flan
77. Cherry Flan
78. Fruit Flan

79. Banana Custard
80. Manchester Tart
81. Cherry Tartlets
82. Custard Tart
83. Chocolate Tart
84. Almond Tart
85. Jam Tart
86. Marmalade Tart
87. Treacle Tart
88. Mince Pies
89. Lemon Meringue Pie
90. Pineapple Upside-Down Cake
91. Pancakes
92. Prunes and Rice
93. Pears and Rice
94. Rice Pudding
95. Queen's Pudding
96. Sponge and Treacle
97. Trifle
98. Chocolate Sponge and Sauce
99. Chocolate Blancmange
100. White Blancmange and Jam
101. Raspberry Mousse
102. Chocolate Mousse
103. Coffee Mousse
104. Lemon Mousse
105. Fruit Salad
106. Fruit Jelly
107. Steamed Sponge Pudding
108. Steamed Fruit Sponge Pudding
109. Steamed Ginger Sponge Pudding
110. Semolina Pudding

4

Sweet Dishes

52. Apple Fritters

12 lb. cooking apples	*1 pint water*
12 eggs	*2 oz. vegetable oil*
2 lb. wholewheat flour	*sea salt*
1 pint milk	

Peel, core, and slice apples. Beat salted flour, eggs, milk and water in the mixer for 12 minutes, speed 3, balloon whisk, add 2 oz. vegetable oil. Dip apple slices in batter and fry in hot vegetable oil.

53. Pineapple Fritters

2 × A10 tins of pineapple slices

Batter and method as in Apple Fritters, recipe 52.

54. Banana Fritters

60 small bananas sliced lengthways

Batter and method as in Apple Fritters, recipe 52.

55. **Apple Pie** (pastry under and over)

14 lb. cooking apples	*3½ lb. margarine*
2 lemons	*3½ lb. lard*
2 lb. Barbados sugar	*1 oz. sea salt*
handful of cloves	*2 pints water*
8 lb. wholewheat flour	*1 egg*

Mix lard into salted flour in the mixer using dough hook and speed 1. Add water gradually, roll out, dot with margarine, fold and roll out again. Line tins with pastry and fill with sliced apples, juice and rind of two lemons and a few cloves, sprinkle sugar all over and cover with remaining pastry. Brush with egg and bake in oven 450° F. or Reg. 8 for 1 hour approx.

56. **Apricot Pie**

16 lb. fresh apricots
or
2 × A10 tins of apricots

Pastry recipe and method as in Apple Pie, recipe 55.

57. **Gooseberry Pie**

16 lb. fresh gooseberries

Pastry recipe and method as in Apple Pie, recipe 55.

58. **Apple Tart**

16 lb. cooking apples	*1½ lb. margarine*
2 lemons	*1½ lb. lard*
2 lb. Barbados sugar	*1 pint water*
4 lb. wholewheat flour	*1 egg*

54

Slice apples and place in deep pie dishes together with sugar, juice and rind of 2 lemons, and a little water. Mix lard into flour in mixer using dough hook, and speed 1. Add water gradually, roll out, dot with margarine, fold and roll out again. Cover pie dishes, brush with egg, and bake in oven 400° F. or Reg. 6 for approx. 1 hour.

59. Blackberry and Apple Tart

14 lb. cooking apples   *2 lb. Barbados sugar*
4 lb. blackberries

Pastry and method as in Apple Tart, recipe 58.

60. Apricot Tart

16 lb. fresh apricots   *2 lb. Barbados sugar*
    or
3 × A10 tins apricots

Pastry and method as in Apple Tart, recipe 58.

61. Gooseberry Tart

16 lb. fresh gooseberries
2 lb. Barbados sugar

Pastry and method as in Apple Tart, recipe 58.

62. Rhubarb Tart

18 lb. fresh rhubarb
2 lb. Barbados sugar

Pastry and method as in Apple Tart, recipe 58.

63. Apple Crunch

16 lb. cooking apples	*5 lb. plain wholewheat flour*
2 lb. Barbados sugar	*2 lb. Barbados sugar*
	2 lb. magarine

Slice apples, place in dishes with Barbados sugar. Mix flour, sugar and margarine together in mixer, spade attachment speed 2. Cover apples with crunch mixture and bake in oven 375° F. or Reg. 5 for 1 hour. The addition of 1 lb. cashew nuts to crunch mixture makes a pleasant and interesting change.

64. Apricot Crunch

As recipe 63 using 16 lb. fresh apricots or 3 × A10 tins.

65. Pineapple Crunch

As recipe 63 using 3 × A10 tins pineapple pieces.

66. Rhubarb Crunch

As recipe 63 using 18 lb. rhubarb.

67. Gooseberry Crunch

As recipe 63 using 16 lb. gooseberries.

68. Plum Crunch

As recipe 63 using 20 lb. plums.

Sweet Dishes

69. Apple Sponge

16 lb. cooking apples	*3 lb. margarine*
2 lb. Barbados sugar	*2 lb. Barbados sugar*
	3 lb. self-raising whole-wheat flour
	15 eggs

Peel and slice apples, place in dishes and sprinkle with sugar. Cream margarine and sugar, add eggs then flour and $\frac{1}{2}$ cup hot water. Spread sponge mixture over apples and bake in oven 400° F. or Reg. 6 for $\frac{3}{4}$ hour.

70. Apricot Sponge

As recipe 69 using 16 lb. fresh apricots or 3 × A10 tins.

71. Apple Meringue

16 lb. cooking apples	MERINGUE
2 lb. Barbados sugar	*12 egg whites*
4 pints milk	*1½ lb. Demerara sugar*
4 oz. custard powder	
12 egg yolks	

Peel, slice and stew apples gently until soft, sweeten. Boil milk in double boiler, mix custard powder to a smooth paste with a little cold milk and add to the boiler, cool a little and add egg yolks. Mix with apples and place in dishes. Whip up egg whites in mixer, balloon whisk and speed 3, add Demerara sugar, spread on top of apple mixture and cook in oven 350° F or Reg. 4 until meringue is crisp.

72. Apricot Meringue

As recipe 71 using 16 lb. fresh apricots or 3 × A10 tins.

73. Pineapple Meringue

As recipe 71 using 3 × A10 tins pinapple pieces.

74. Baked Apples

18 lb. cooking apples   *1 lb. sultanas or raisins*
2 lb. Barbados sugar

Wash and core apples, fill with sultanas or raisins and Barbados sugar. Place in shallow dishes in a little water, sprinkle some extra sugar in the water to make a nice syrup and bake in oven 350° F. or Reg. 4 for approx. 1 hour.

75. Stewed Apples

18 lb. cooking apples   *4 pints water*
2 lb. Barbados sugar

Peel, slice and cook the apples in 4 pints water for approx. $\frac{3}{4}$ hour. Remove from heat and add sugar.

76. Apricot Flan

10 lb. fresh stewed apricots   GLAZE
   or   *4 pints fruit juice*
2 × A10 tins apricot halves   *4 tbs. arrowroot*
3 lb. margarine
1½ lb. Barbados sugar   MOCK CREAM
15 eggs   *1 lb. butter*
3 lb. self-raising whole-   *8 oz. Barbados sugar*
   wheat flour   *1 cup milk powder*

Cream margarine and sugar, add eggs, then flour and $\frac{1}{2}$ cup hot water, bake in oven 400° F. or Reg. 6 for 30 minutes. When sponge is cool place apricot halves on top. Mix arrowroot to a smooth paste with a little cold fruit juice, add to hot juice and boil until clear. When cool pour over apricots and when set decorate flan with mock cream.

77. Cherry Flan

As recipe 76 using 12 lb. fresh cherries washed and stoned or 2 × A10 tins.

78. Fruit Flan

As recipe 76 using:

1 × A10 tin mandarins	*1 × 2-lb. tin pineapple*
1 × 2-lb. tin cherries or	*pieces*
2 lb. fresh	*2 lb. fresh grapes*

79. Banana Custard

14 lb. bananas	*10 oz. custard powder*
3 lb. raspberry jam	*8 oz. Barbados sugar*
12 pints milk	*2 oz. soya flour*

Bring milk to the boil in double saucepan, mix custard powder and soya flour to a smooth paste with a little cold milk, add to saucepan, add sugar and cool. Slice bananas into dishes, spread with raspberry jam and cover with custard sauce.

Mixing 2 oz. soya flour with the custard powder adds greatly to the food value. Soya flour has a very high protein content.

80. Manchester Tart

4 lb. wholewheat flour	Sponge Mixture
1½ lb. margarine	*3 lb. self-raising whole-*
1½ lb. lard	*wheat flour*
1 pint water	*2 lb. margarine*
sea salt	*2 lb. Barbados sugar*
3 lb. raspberry jam	*15 eggs*

Mix lard into salted flour in mixer using dough hook and speed 1. Roll out, dot with margarine, fold and roll out again. Line tins with pastry then spread with jam. Cream sugar and margarine together in mixer with spade attachment speed 3, add eggs and flour and a little boiling water. Pour sponge mixture over jam and bake in oven 400° F. or Reg. 6 for 40 minutes.

81. Cherry Tartlets

FLAN PASTRY	GLAZE
4 lb. plain wholewheat flour	*2 pints fruit juice*
2 lb. margarine	*2 tbs. arrowroot*
8 oz. Barbados sugar	*6 oz. Barbados sugar*
6 eggs	
½ pint water	MOCK CREAM
	½ lb. butter
1 × A10 tin cherries	*4 oz. Barbados sugar*
or	*½ cup milk powder*
10 lb. fresh cherries	

Make pastry by mixing flour, margarine and sugar in mixer using dough hook and speed 1, add water and eggs to make soft dough, roll out and line tins. Prick and bake in oven 400° F. or Reg. 6 for ½ hour, cool and fill with stoned fruit. Make glaze by dissolving sugar in fruit juice and boiling for 5 minutes. Add arrowroot mixed to a smooth paste first with a little cold juice and boil for a further 2 minutes, stirring all the time until the mixture is clear, pour over fruit and decorate with mock cream.

82. Custard Tart

24 eggs	FLAN PASTRY
8 pints milk	*As in cherry tartlets,*
12 oz. Barbados sugar	*recipe 81*

Line tins with flan pastry. Make custard by beating eggs and adding warmed milk and sugar. Pour custard into pastry tins and bake in oven 350° F. or Reg. 4 for 20 minutes.

83. Chocolate Tart

10 pints milk	Flan Pastry
12 oz. cornflour	*As in recipe 81 for cherry*
8 oz. cocoa	*tartlets*
1 lb. Barbados sugar	

Bring 8 pints of milk to the boil in double saucepan. Mix cornflour, sugar and cocoa to a smooth paste with 2 pints of cold milk and add to the double saucepan, cook all together for a further 10 minutes. Line tins with flan pastry, pour in chocolate filling and bake in oven 350° F. or Reg. 4 for 40 minutes.

84. Almond Tart

2 lb. margarine	Flan Pastry
1½ lb. Barbados sugar	*As in recipe 81 for cherry*
18 eggs	*tartlets*
2 lb. Scotch oat flakes	*5 lb. raspberry jam*
few drops almond essence	

Cream margarine and sugar in beater using spade attachment and speed 3, add eggs and oats and finally a few drops of almond essence. Line tins with flan pastry, spread with jam, pour almond filling on top and bake in oven 400° F. or Reg. 6 for 40 minutes.

85. Jam Tart

4 lb. plain wholewheat flour	*1 pint water*
1½ lb. margarine	*sea salt*
1½ lb. lard	*5 lb. jam*

Mix lard into salted flour in mixer using dough hook and speed 1, add water gradually, roll out, dot with margarine, fold and roll out again. Line tins with pastry spread with jam, decorate with pastry strips and bake in oven 400° F. or Reg. 6 for 40 minutes.

86. Marmalade Tart

As for Jam Tart recipe 85, using 5 lb. marmalade instead of jam.

87. Treacle Tart

$2\frac{1}{2}$ *lb. wholewheat bread-*
crumbs
14 lb. golden syrup
juice and rind of 3 lemons

PASTRY
As for jam tart, recipe 85

Melt syrup, mix with breadcrumbs, add lemon juice and rind. Line tins with pastry, pour in syrup mixture, decorate with pastry strips and bake in oven 450° F. or Reg. 8 for 40 minutes.

88. Mince Pies

8 lb. plain wholewheat flour
$3\frac{1}{2}$ lb. lard
$3\frac{1}{2}$ lb. margarine

2 pints water (approx.)
sea salt
7 lb. mincemeat
1 egg

Mix lard into salted flour in mixer using dough hook and speed 1, add water gradually, roll out, dot with margarine, fold and roll out again. Line patty tins, fill with mincemeat, cover with pastry, brush with egg and bake in oven 400° F. or Reg. 6 for $\frac{1}{2}$ hour.

89. Lemon Meringue Pie

14 oz. cornflour
4 pints water
1½ lb. Barbados sugar
18 egg yolks
18 lemons
4 oz. margarine

FLAN PASTRY
As in recipe 81 for cherry
tartlets

MERINGUE
18 egg whites
2 lb. Demerara sugar

Line tins with flan pastry and bake blind for 30 minutes in oven 400° F. or Reg. 5. Boil water, lemon juice and rind together, add cornflour mixed to a smooth paste with cold water and boil for a further 5 minutes stirring all the time. Remove from heat, add sugar, margarine and egg yolks. Pour mixture into pastry cases, whip up egg whites with Demerara sugar in mixer, balloon whisk speed 3, until stiff, cover lemon filling and bake in oven 350° F. or Reg. 4 for 1½ hours or until meringue is crisp.

90. Pineapple Upside-Down Cake

3 lb. margarine
1½ lb. Barbados sugar
15 eggs
3 lb. self-raising whole-
wheat flour
1 cup pineapple juice

1 × A10-tin pineapple
pieces
1 lb. Barbados sugar
1 lb. margarine

Cream margarine and sugar in mixer with spade attachment speed 3, add eggs, then flour and pineapple juice. Sprinkle pineapple pieces, sugar and margarine over the base of baking tins, pour sponge mixture on top and bake in oven 400° F. or Reg. 6 for ½ hour. Turn upside-down and serve with custard.

Sweet Dishes

91. Pancakes

4 lb. plain wholewheat flour	1 pint vegetable oil
18 eggs	3 lb. Demerara sugar
7 pints milk	10 lemons

Beat flour, eggs, and milk in mixer, balloon whisk, speed 3, for 12 minutes, pour into jugs. Grease frying-pans with hot vegetable oil, pour a little batter into frying-pan and cook for a few minutes on each side. Serve with Demerara sugar and lemon wedges.

92. Prunes and Rice

8 lb. prunes	3 lb. natural brown rice
12 oz. Barbados sugar	2 lb. Barbados sugar
	16 pints milk

Soak prunes overnight, stew gently until soft, approx. 1 hour, add sugar. Cook rice in double boiler with milk and sugar for approx. 2 hours.

93. Pears and Rice

16 lb. fresh pears	3 lb. natural brown rice
1 lb. Barbados sugar	2 lb. Barbados sugar
	16 pints milk

Skin, core, and stew pears gently until soft, add sugar. Cook rice in double boiler with the milk and sugar for approx. 2 hours.

94. Rice Pudding

$2\frac{1}{2}$ lb. natural brown rice	2 × 12-oz. tins evaporated
$1\frac{1}{2}$ lb. Barbados sugar	milk
20 pints milk	

Put washed rice in pie dishes, add sugar, fill up with milk and cook in oven 350° F. or Reg. 4 for 2 hours approx.

95. Queen's Pudding

3 lb. wholemeal bread-
crumbs
12 pints milk
18 egg yolks
10 oz. Barbados sugar
4 lb. raspberry jam
rind of 3 lemons

MERINGUE
18 egg whites
2 lb. Demerara sugar

Place breadcrumbs and lemon rind in dishes, heat the milk in double boiler, add egg yolks, sugar, pour over breadcrumbs and bake in oven 375° F. or Reg. 5 for 30 minutes or until firm. Beat up egg whites in mixer, balloon whisk speed 3, add Demerara sugar. Spread jam over crumb mixture and cover with meringue, replace in oven 350° F. or Reg. 4 for 45 minutes or until meringue is crisp.

96. Sponge and Treacle

3 lb. margarine
1½ lb. Barbados sugar
15 eggs

3 lb. self-raising whole-
wheat flour
4 lb. golden syrup

Cream margarine and sugar together, add eggs, then flour, add ½ cup hot water and place mixture in greased and floured tins. Bake in oven 400° F. or Reg. 6 for 30 minutes. Heat syrup and serve in jugs.

97. Trifle

3 lb. margarine
1½ lb. Barbados sugar
15 eggs

3 lb. self-raising whole-
wheat flour
4 lb. raspberry jam

12 pints milk	MOCK CREAM
8 oz. Barbados sugar	*1 lb. butter*
16 oz. custard powder	*8 oz. Barbados sugar*
8 oz. blanched almonds	*1 cup milk powder*
1 lb. glacé cherries	

Cream margarine and sugar together, add eggs, then flour, add ½ cup hot water and place in greased and floured tins, bake in oven 400° F. or Reg. 6 for 30 minutes. Bring milk to the boil in double saucepan, mix custard powder to a smooth paste with a little cold milk, add to double saucepan, add sugar. Spread sponge with jam, cut into small pieces, place in dishes and cover with custard sauce. Decorate with mock cream, cherries and almonds.

98. Chocolate Sponge and Chocolate Sauce

3 lb. margarine	SAUCE
1½ lb. Barbados sugar	*8 pints milk*
15 eggs	*8 oz. cornflour*
2½ lb. self-raising whole-	*8 oz. cocoa*
wheat flour	*8 oz. Barbados sugar*
8 oz. cocoa	*8 oz. margarine*

Cream margarine and sugar, add eggs, then cocoa and flour, add ½ cup hot water and place in greased and floured tins. Bake in oven 400° F. or Reg. 6 for 30 minutes. Boil milk in double boiler, mix cornflour to a smooth paste with a little cold milk and add to the boiler, add sugar, cocoa, and margarine and boil for 10 minutes.

99. Chocolate Blancmange

12 pints milk	*12 oz. Barbados sugar*
16 oz. cornflour	*8 oz. margarine*
8 oz. cocoa	

Bring milk to the boil in double saucepan, mix cornflour to a smooth paste with a little cold milk and add to the saucepan, add sugar, cocoa and margarine, cook all together for 10 minutes or until thick, pour into oiled moulds.

100. White Blancmange and Jam

12 pints milk
16 oz. cornflour
7 lb. raspberry jam

12 oz. Barbados sugar
8 oz. margarine

As recipe 99 leaving out the cocoa. Serve jam separately.

101. Raspberry Mousse

12 × ½-pint tins evaporated milk
3 lb. fresh raspberries or
3 × 16-oz. tins

8 oz. Barbados sugar
4 oz. gelatine

Boil tins of milk for 20 minutes before opening, cool in refrigerator. Beat milk, three tins at a time, in mixer using balloon whisk and speed 3. Heat sugar and raspberries, then sprinkle gelatine over the top stirring until dissolved. Add one-third of this mixture to milk in mixer and continue beating for 2 minutes. Pour into glass dishes and repeat this procedure twice more. Place in refrigerator until ready to serve.

102. Chocolate Mousse

As recipe 101 using 12 oz. cocoa and 1 pint water instead of raspberries.

103. Coffee Mousse

As recipe 101 using 4 oz. Nescafé and 1 pint water instead of raspberries.

104. Lemon Mousse

As recipe 101 using fruit, juice and finely-grated rind of 16
lemons plus ½ pint water instead of raspberries.

105. Fruit Salad

1 × A10-tin pears	*12 oranges*
1 × A10-tin peach slices	*12 bananas*
1 × A10-tin pineapple	*1 melon and 2 lb. grapes*
pieces	*for party occasions*
12 eating apples	

Discard syrup from tinned fruit and make a natural syrup with
4 pints water and 1 lb. honey or 8 oz. Barbados sugar. Mix all
fruit together in large bowl and chill before serving.

106. Fruit Jelly

1 × A10-tin of either	*3 lb. 12 oz. jelly powder*
pineapple pieces	*2 gallons water*
mandarins or raspberries	

Dissolve powder in 1 gallon boiling water and make up to 2
gallons with tin of fruit and cold water. Pour into oiled
moulds.

107. Steamed Sponge Pudding

3 lb. margarine	*7 lb. jam*
1½ lb. Barbados sugar	*or*
4 lb. self-raising whole-	*7 lb. marmalade*
wheat flour	*or*
24 eggs	*4 lb. golden syrup*
¼ pint milk	

68

Cream margarine and sugar together in mixer using spade attachment speed 3, add eggs, then flour and milk. Place in well-greased bowls, cover with grease-proof paper and steam for 2 hours. Serve with jam, marmalade or golden syrup.

108. Steamed Fruit Sponge Pudding

As recipe 107 for Steamed Sponge adding 2 lb. sultanas.

109. Steamed Ginger Sponge Pudding

As recipe 107 for Steamed Sponge adding 4 oz. ground ginger.

110. Semolina Pudding

3 gallons milk   *2 lb. Barbados sugar*
3 lb. wholewheat semolina

Boil milk in double boiler, mix semolina with little cold milk and add to boiler, add sugar and boil for 1 hour.

Chapter 5

SUPPER DISHES

111. Spaghetti Cheese
112. Cauliflower Cheese
113. Cheese Pudding
114. Potato Cheese and Bacon Pie
115. Poached Eggs on Mashed Potatoes with Cheese Sauce
116. Welsh Rarebit
117. Potato Cakes and Bacon
118. Fried Eggs on Baked Beans
119. Bacon Beans and Sauté Potatoes
120. Scotch Woodcock
121. Curried Eggs and Rice
122. Scotch Eggs
123. Mushroom Patties
124. Herrings
125. Herring Roes on Toast
126. Sardine Salad
127. Egg Mayonnaise
128. Mushrooms on Toast
129. Minced Ham on Toast
130. Minced Chicken on Toast
131. Sausages on Spaghetti

132. Spaghetti Bolognaise
133. Savoury Meat Balls
134. Fried Rice
135. Quiche Lorraine
136. Sausage Rolls
137. Sausage Casserole
138. Baked Lasagne
139. Meat Fritters
140. Savoury Pancakes
141. Cold Meat and Salad
142. Hamburgers
143. Hot Dogs

5

Supper Dishes

111. Spaghetti Cheese

*4 lb. long spaghetti (whole-
 wheat)*
1 lb. margarine
12 pints milk

*16 oz. plain wholewheat
 flour*
3 lb. grated Cheddar cheese
sea salt
pepper

Break spaghetti into boiling salted water and cook for 20 minutes, strain and wash. Bring 11 pints milk to the boil in double saucepan, add flour mixed to a smooth paste with 1 pint cold milk, cook for a further 5 minutes, add margarine, cheese and seasoning. Pour sauce onto spaghetti, mix well and place in dishes, sprinkle with grated cheese and put under the grill for a few minutes until brown.

112. Cauliflower Cheese

12 large cauliflowers
12 pints cheese sauce as in recipe 111 for spaghetti

Cook cauliflowers in boiling salted water, for 15 minutes remove from water whilst still firm, break into small pieces, place in dishes and cover with cheese sauce. Grill.

113. Cheese Pudding

16 pints milk	*3 lb. grated Cheddar cheese*
1 lb. margarine	*24 eggs*
16 oz. plain wholewheat flour	*sea salt, pepper*

Bring to the boil 15 pints milk in double saucepan, add flour mixed to a smooth paste with 1 pint cold milk and cook for a further 5 minutes, add cheese, margarine and seasoning, remove from heat and add the egg yolks. Beat up egg whites in mixer, balloon attachment speed 3, until stiff, fold into white sauce, pour into pie dishes and bake in oven 400° F. or Reg. 6 for 45 minutes or until firm and risen, serve promptly.

114. Potato Cheese and Bacon Pie

20 lb. cooked potatoes	*12 pints cheese sauce as in*
3 lb. onions	*spaghetti recipe 111*
3 lb. streaky bacon	*6 oz. chopped parsley*

Grill bacon. Slice potatoes into dishes, sprinkle with chopped parsley, bacon and onions, cover with cheese sauce and grill.

115. Poached Eggs on Mashed Potatoes with Cheese Sauce

15 lb. potatoes	CHEESE SAUCE
1 pint milk	*8 pints milk*
8 oz. margarine	*1½ lb. Cheddar cheese*
60 eggs	*8 oz. wholewheat flour*
parsley	*8 oz. margarine*
	salt
	pepper

Cook and mash potatoes, season well and place in dishes.

Poach eggs, place on top of potatoes. Boil 7 pints of milk in double boiler, mix flour to smooth paste with 1 pint cold milk and add to double boiler, add margarine and grated cheese, season well and pour over eggs. Decorate dish with parsley sprigs.

116. Welsh Rarebit

4 lb. grated Cheddar cheese   *5 × 2-lb. wholewheat loaves*
12 oz. melted margarine
2 pints milk
dash of Worcester sauce
salt
pepper

Mix all ingredients, season well. Slice bread, toast lightly, spread with mixture and place under grill.

117. Potato Cakes and Bacon

15 lb. potatoes   *2 lb. wholewheat bread-*
1 pint milk   *crumbs*
8 oz. margarine   *8 eggs*
3 lb. streaky bacon   *salt*
   pepper

Cook potatoes and mash with milk and margarine, season well, shape into flat cakes. Egg and breadcrumb the cakes and deep fry in oil. Grill bacon for 5 minutes and serve one slice on top of each cake.

118. Fried Eggs on Baked Beans

60 eggs   *3 × A10-tins baked beans*
   in tomato sauce

Heat beans in double boiler, place on dishes and put fried eggs on top.

119. Bacon Beans and Sauté Potatoes

3 lb. streaky bacon
15 lb. cooked potatoes

2 × A10-tins beans in
tomato sauce
2 lb. margarine

Heat beans in double boiler, slice cooked potatoes and sauté in margarine. Grill bacon for 5 minutes. Put beans in centre of dish with bacon on top and surround with sauté potatoes.

120. Scotch Woodcock

60 eggs
2 pints milk
1 lb. margarine
sea salt
pepper

5 × 2-lb. wholewheat loaves
1 bottle anchovy essence
1 lb. margarine

Beat eggs with milk and margarine, season and cook in double boiler for approx. 1 hour. Toast 60 slices of bread and spread with margarine and anchovy essence, pile scrambled egg on toast.

121. Curried Eggs and Rice

60 eggs
5 lb. natural brown rice

8 pints milk
12 oz. wholewheat flour
1 lb. margarine
4 oz. curry powder

Hard boil the eggs. Cook rice in boiling salted water for 20 minutes. Bring the milk to the boil in double saucepan, mix flour to a smooth paste with a little cold milk and add to double saucepan, cook for a further few minutes and add margarine and curry powder. Put eggs in centre of dish surrounded by rice but serve sauce separately.

122. Scotch Eggs

60 hard-boiled eggs	*8 eggs*
10 lb. sausage meat	*½ pint milk*
1 lb. wholewheat flour	*1 lb. wholewheat bread-crumbs*

Shell eggs, dip in flour, divide sausage meat into 60 portions and cover eggs with sausage meat. Dip in eggs and milk, then breadcrumbs, and fry in vegetable oil.

123. Mushroom Patties

3 lb. mushrooms	*4 lb. wholewheat flour*
6 pints milk	*1½ lb. lard*
10 oz. wholewheat flour	*1½ lb. margarine*
8 oz. margarine	*1 pint water*
	sea salt

Bring 5 pints milk to the boil in double saucepan, add flour mixed to a smooth paste with 1 pint cold milk, add margarine and cook all together for further 5 minutes. Slice mushrooms and fry gently, add to sauce, season well. Mix lard into salted flour in mixer using dough hook, speed 1, sprinkle in water, roll out, dot with margarine, fold, roll out again. Line patty tins with pastry and bake in oven 400° F. or Reg. 6 for ½ hour. Fill cases with mushroom filling and serve with mashed potatoes and sliced tomatoes.

124. Herrings

60 boned herrings

Wash, scale, cut off head and tails. Dip in seasoned flour and fry in vegetable oil or place in well-greased tins and bake in oven 375° F. or Reg. 5 for ¾ hour.

125. Herring Roes on Toast

16 lb. herring roes   *5 × 2-lb. wholewheat loaves*
8 eggs
1 lb. wholewheat bread-
*   crumbs*

Dip the roes in egg and breadcrumbs and fry gently in vegetable oil, serve on toast.

126. Sardine Salad

8 lb. sardines   *2 cucumbers*
12 lettuce   *30 hard-boiled eggs*
3 lb. tomatoes   *1½ lb. watercress*

127. Egg Mayonnaise

60 eggs   *1 pint salad cream*
12 lettuce   *paprika*
3 lb. tomatoes

Hard boil eggs, cover with salad cream and sprinkle with paprika. Serve with lettuce and tomatoes.

128. Mushrooms on Toast

4 lb. mushrooms   *4 pints milk*
5 × 2-lb. wholewheat loaves   *8 oz. margarine*
sea salt, pepper   *10 oz. wholewheat flour*

Slice and fry mushrooms gently. Boil 3 pints milk in double boiler, add flour mixed to smooth paste with 1 pint cold milk, add margarine and mushrooms, season well and serve on toast.

129. Minced Ham on Toast

2 × 7-lb. hock	2 pints milk
5 × 2-lb. wholewheat loaves	4 oz. margarine
	5 oz. wholewheat flour

Cover hock with water and simmer for approx. 2 hours, remove, and mince. Heat 1 pint milk to boiling point, add flour mixed to smooth paste with 1 pint cold milk, add margarine. Stir sauce into ham and serve on toast.

130. Minced Chicken on Toast

2 chickens	2 pints milk
5 × 2-lb. wholewheat loaves	4 oz. margarine
sea salt, pepper	5 oz. wholewheat flour

Cover chickens with water and simmer gently for $1\frac{1}{2}$ hours approx. Remove and mince. Heat 1 pint milk to boiling point, add flour mixed to a smooth paste with 1 pint cold milk, add margarine and chicken, season well and serve on toast.

131. Sausages on Spaghetti

8 lb. pork sausages (8 to lb.)	4 oz. chopped parsley
3 × A10-tins spaghetti in tomato sauce	

Lay sausages on greased trays and grill for 15 minutes approx. Heat spaghetti in double boiler, place in dishes with sausages on top, garnish with chopped parsley.

132. Spaghetti Bolognaise

6 lb. minced beef	3 pints tomato sauce
4 onions	2 pints gravy
4 lb. tomatoes	6 lb. long spaghetti
sea salt	4 oz. chopped parsley
pepper	
garlic salt	

Cook spaghetti in boiling salted water for 15 minutes, drain and wash. Cook mince for 1 hour. Fry onions and tomatoes, add to mince, stir in tomato sauce and gravy, season and pour over spaghetti before serving, sprinkle with parsley.

133. Savoury Meat Balls

12 lb. minced beef or left-overs	8 eggs
4 lb. mashed potatoes	1 pint milk
6 eggs	2 lb. wholewheat bread-crumbs
4 oz. chopped parsley	
garlic salt	

Mix mince, potatoes, parsley, eggs and garlic salt, form into balls, dip in eggs and milk, then breadcrumbs. Deep fry in vegetable oil. Serve with sliced tomatoes.

134. Fried Rice

5 lb. natural brown rice	2 lb. carrots
2 lb. meat leftovers	2 peppers
3 lb. tomatoes	8 oz. chopped parsley
2 lb. mushrooms	1 pint vegetable oil
2 lb. onions	1 lb. butter

Cook rice in boiling salted water for 20 minutes, drain and

wash. Fry rice in a mixture of oil and butter until faintly coloured, place in large bowl. Fry sliced mushrooms, peppers, onions, carrots and tomatoes and mix together with meat leftovers, stir into rice and sprinkle with parsley.

135. Quiche Lorraine

4 lb. wholewheat flour	*3 lb. onions*
1½ lb. lard	*3 lb. tomatoes*
1½ lb. margarine	*3 lb. bacon*
1 pint water	*2 lb. grated Cheddar cheese*
sea salt	*2 pints milk*
	24 eggs
	8 oz. chopped parsley

Mix lard into salted flour, add water gradually, roll out, dot with margarine, fold and roll out again. Line tins with pastry and bake blind in oven 400° F. or Reg. 6 until dry. Fry chopped bacon, tomatoes and onions, sprinkle over pastry, beat eggs into milk, pour over mixture, then the grated cheese and finally the parsley. Bake in oven 400° F. or Reg. 6 for 30 minutes or place under medium grill for 5 minutes.

136. Sausage Rolls

4 lb. wholewheat flour	*1 pint water*
1½ lb. lard	*sea salt*
1½ lb. margarine	*5 lb. pork sausage meat*

Mix lard into salted flour in mixer using dough hook speed 1, add water gradually, roll out, dot with margarine, fold and roll out again into oblong shapes, cut into strips. Roll out sausage meat and place rolls along pastry strips, moisten edges with water and fold over, brush with egg and cut into required lengths, bake in oven 425° F. or Reg. 7 for 30 minutes.

137. Sausage Casserole

8 lb. pork sausages	16 pints stock or soup
4 lb. carrots	16 oz. wholewheat flour
4 lb. onions	4 Oxo cubes
4 lb. tomatoes	1 tbs. Marmite
4 peppers	garlic salt
	sea salt
	pepper
	chopped parsley

Grill sausages lightly and place in casseroles. Fry onions, carrots, tomatoes and peppers and add to casseroles. Thicken stock, flavour and pour into casseroles, bake in oven 400° F. or Reg. 6, for 1 hour.

138. Baked Lasagne

10 lb. minced beef	5 lb. flat noodles
sea salt	2 lb. cottage cheese
pepper	or
garlic salt	2 lb. grated Cheddar cheese
4 lb. tomatoes	10 eggs
1 pint tomato sauce	4 oz. chopped parsley
	large packet cheese slices

Brown meat in oil, add seasonings, sliced tomatoes, and tomato sauce and simmer in uncovered pan until thick, approx. 1 hour, stirring occasionally. Cook noodles in boiling salted water. Mix cottage cheese, eggs and chopped parsley, layer noodles and cheese mixture into dishes, lay cheese slices over the top and cover with meat mixture, bake in oven 375° F. or Reg. 5 for 1 hour.

139. Meat Fritters

9 lb. luncheon meat   sea salt
2 lb. wholewheat flour   3 pints milk
18 eggs   ½ cup olive oil

Mix flour, salt, eggs and milk in mixer and beat for 12
minutes, add olive oil. Slice luncheon meat, dip in batter and
fry. Serve with sauté potatoes or baked beans.

140. Savoury Pancakes

3 lb. wholewheat flour   3 lb. mushrooms
16 eggs   3 lb. streaky bacon
5 pints milk   3 lb. tomatoes
sea salt   4 oz. chopped parsley

Mix flour, salt, eggs and milk in mixer and beat for 12
minutes, pour into jugs. Slice and fry mushrooms, tomatoes
and bacon, add parsley. Cook ten large pancakes in heavy
frying-pan, fill with savoury mixture and divide each pancake
into six, serve with tomato sauce.

141. Cold Ham   Luncheon Meat   Corned Beef

18 lb. hock   9 lb. luncheon meat   9 lb. corned beef
Serve with salad:

12 lettuces   3 lb. tomatoes   2 cucumbers
16 hard-boiled eggs   1 lb. watercress

142. Hamburgers

60 hamburger wholewheat   3 lb. onions
    rolls   French mustard
60 hamburger steaks

Fry steaks and onions, spread rolls with mustard and fill with steaks and onions, put on trays in warm oven until required. Serve with tomato sauce.

143. Hot Dogs

60 long-shaped wholewheat   3 lb. onions
*   rolls   French mustard*
60 pork sausages

Grill sausages, fry onions. Spread rolls with mustard and fill with sausages and onions, put on trays in warm oven until required. Serve with tomato sauce.

Chapter 6

SOUPS

144. Oxtail Soup
145. Scotch Broth
146. Vegetable Soup
147. Potato Soup
148. Pea Soup
149. Cream of Celery Soup
150. Cream of Chicken Soup
151. Cream of Mushroom Soup
152. Tomato Soup
153. Lentil Soup
154. Basic Stock

6

Soups

144. Oxtail Soup

4 oxtails	2 gallons water or stock
12 onions	large bouquet garni
18 carrots	12 peppercorns
1 head of celery	12 oz. wholewheat flour

Wash oxtails, well cover with water and simmer for 3 hours, remove scum and allow to cool, remove fat. Fry vegetables in vegetable oil, add to the stock together with the bouquet garni, peppercorns, sea salt and pepper. Simmer for a further hour, add flour mixed to a smooth paste with a little cold water and boil for 10 minutes.

145. Scotch Broth

10 lb. neck of mutton	10 carrots
20 pints water or stock	10 onions
1 lb. pearl barley	10 turnips
6 bay leaves	4 oz. chopped parlsey
sea salt	garlic salt
pepper	

Remove fat and skin from meat, cover with water and simmer for 1 hour, remove scum, cool and remove fat. Add vegetables and seasoning and simmer for a further hour, remove the bones, take off the meat and return meat to saucepan, add chopped parsley and serve.

Soups

146. Vegetable Soup

4 lb. peas	½ lb. butter
2 lb. mushrooms	10 oz. wholewheat flour
3 head celery	16 pints milk
3 lb. carrots	4 pints stock
2 lb. onions	salt
	pepper
	bouquet garni

Wash and dice the vegetables, put in large saucepan with butter, cook with lid on over gentle heat for 15 minutes, sprinkle with flour and fry a little, add milk and stock gradually, stirring all the time, add bouquet garni, season well and simmer until all the vegetables are tender.

147. Potato Soup

10 lb. potatoes	pepper
4 lb. onions	1 tbs. ground nutmeg
4 lb. leeks	bouquet garni
4 oz. chopped parlsey	10 pints milk
sea salt	10 pints stock

Peel and cut up potatoes, onions and leeks, cover with milk and stock and simmer until soft, put through a sieve, return to saucepan, bring to the boil, add bouquet garni, nutmeg, salt and pepper, simmer for 15 minutes, add chopped parsley and serve.

148. Pea Soup

16 lb. peas	16 pints water or stock
3 lb. onions	sea salt
8 oz. grated Cheddar cheese	pepper
4 oz. chopped mint	12 oz. wholewheat flour
	8 pints milk

Boil peas in their pods in 16 pints of water or stock together with the onions. When cooked put through the sieve together with the water they are cooked in, return to the saucepan, add milk and flour mixed to a smooth paste with a little cold milk, simmer and stir for 5 minutes, add mint and serve with grated cheese.

149. Cream of Celery Soup

8 heads celery	*bouquet garni*
20 pints milk	*sea salt*
½ lb. butter	*pepper*
16 oz. wholewheat flour	

Melt butter in large saucepan, gently sauté diced celery, add flour and milk and bring to the boil, add bouquet garni, seasoning, and simmer for a further 15 minutes.

150. Cream of Chicken Soup

1 boiling fowl	*2 heads celery*
20 pints water	*½ lb. butter*
16 oz. wholewheat flour	*sea salt*
4 oz. chopped parsley	*pepper*

Cover chicken with 20 pints water and simmer gently for 2 hours. Chop celery finely and sauté in butter in large saucepan, add flour, then chicken stock. When thick cook for 15 minutes, add chicken meat, parsley, seasoning and serve.

151. Cream of Mushroom Soup

12 lb. mushrooms	*sea salt*
20 pints milk and stock	*pepper*
12 oz. wholewheat flour	*1 lb. butter*
bouquet garni	

Soups

Wash and slice mushrooms, fry gently in butter, add flour, milk and stock. Simmer until thick, add bouquet garni, salt and pepper and simmer for a further 15 minutes.

152. Tomato Soup

20 pints water or stock	12 oz. wholewheat flour
3 lb. carrots	bouquet garni
3 lb. onions	sea salt
1 lb. butter	pepper
4 lb. tomatoes	2 pints tomato purée
½ lb. streaky bacon	

Fry bacon in butter, chop and add carrots, onions and tomatoes. Add flour, seasoning, bouquet garni and tomato purée, then gradually add the stock and bring to the boil. Simmer for 2 hours, strain, reheat and serve.

153. Lentil Soup

3 lb. lentils	1 lb. carrots
3 oz. tomato purée	1 lb. onions
20 pints stock	1 lb. leeks
bouquet garni	2 heads celery
sea salt	1 ham bone
pepper	

Boil all the ingredients in the stock in a large saucepan with the bouquet garni and the ham bone and simmer for 2 hours, strain, reheat and serve.

154. Stock

Stock can be made from leftovers: pieces of meat, bones, bacon rinds, poultry, and any vegetables except potatoes, simmered in water for several hours.

Chapter 7

SALADS AND SANDWICH FILLINGS

155. Potato Salad
156. Spanish Salad
157. Raw Vegetable Salad
158. Lettuce Salad
159. Cauliflower Salad
160. Tomato Salad
161. Green Salad
162. Salade Niçoise
163. Beetroot Salad
164. Cucumber Salad
165. Russian Salad
166. Chicory Salad
167. Banana and Walnut Salad
168. Celery Salad
169. Celery and Egg Salad

Sandwich Fillings

170. Sardine and Tomato
171. Liver Pâté and Cucumber
172. Ham—Eggs—Chives
173. Honey and Nut

174. Marmite and Watercress
175. Bacon
176. Cheese and Celery
177. Curried Egg
178. Banana and Walnut
179. Cheese and Tomato
180. Peanut Butter and Cucumber or Celery
181. Dried Fruit and Nut
182. Anchovy and Egg
183. Peanut Butter and Soya Flour

*   *   *

Homemade Salad Cream [see page 100]

7

Salads and Sandwich Fillings

155. Potato Salad

8 lb. potatoes	2 pints salad cream
½ lb. onions	4 oz. chopped parsley

Boil potatoes and chop into small cubes. Chop onions and parsley, mix together with the potatoes, stir in the salad cream.

156. Spanish Salad

5 lb. tomatoes	4 oz. vegetable oil
2 lb. onions	2 oz. apple cider vinegar
6 green peppers	garlic salt
	sea salt
	pepper

Slice tomatoes and onions. Remove seeds and pith from inside peppers, slice and mix with tomatoes and onions. Sprinkle with dressing.

157. Raw Vegetable Salad

3 heads of celery	4 oz. vegetable oil
3 lb. carrots	2 oz. apple cider vinegar
3 lb. tomatoes	garlic salt
3 cucumbers	sea salt
1 dutch cabbage	pepper

Wash all vegetables, cut in small pieces and toss together in dressing.

158. Lettuce Salad

12 lettuce	*3 cucumbers*
3 lb. tomatoes	*½ lb. watercress*
1 lb. cooked beetroot	*4 bundles radishes*

Wash all vegetables well, arrange lettuce as the base and decorate with other vegetables. Serve with salad cream or french dressing.

159. Cauliflower Salad

8 cauliflowers	*1 pint sald cream*
2 lb. tomatoes	*sea salt*
4 oz. chopped parsley	*paprika*

Break cauliflower heads into small flowerettes. Wash and chop tomatoes. Mix with cauliflower and parsley. Stir in salad cream, sprinkle with paprika.

160. Tomato Salad

8 lb. tomatoes	*3 oz. vegetable oil*
4 oz. chopped parsley	*1½ oz. apple cider vinegar*
2 oz. chopped chives	*garlic salt*
	sea salt
	pepper

Wash tomatoes, slice, season, and sprinkle with chopped parsley, chives and french dressing

161. Green Salad

8 lettuce	*4 oz. vegetable oil*
8 bundles watercress	*2 oz. apple cider vinegar*
4 oz. chopped chives	*garlic salt*
	sea salt
	pepper

Wash vegetables well and toss in french dressing.

162. Salade Niçoise

8 lettuce	*6 × 4-oz. cans tuna fish*
4 green peppers	*4 oz. fresh herbs*
4 lb. tomatoes	
2 cloves garlic	Dressing
12 hard-boiled eggs	*8 oz. vegetable oil*
2 × 2-oz. tins anchovy	*4 oz. apple cider vinegar*
fillets	*sea salt*
1½ lb. cold, cooked rice	*pepper*

Remove seed and pith from inside peppers, slice finely. Wash and separate lettuce. Wash and chop tomatoes. Rub large bowl with garlic cloves and put in the dressing. Toss peppers, lettuce, tomatoes, rice, chopped eggs, fish, and herbs in dressing and decorate with anchovy fillets.

163. Beetroot Salad

12 lb. cooked beetroot	*3 oz. vegetable oil*
2 oz. caraway seeds	*1½ oz. apple cider vinegar*
4 oz. chopped parsley	*garlic salt*
	sea salt
	pepper

Slice beetroot finely, mix with caraway seeds and dressing and sprinkle with parsley.

164. Cucumber Salad

8 cucumbers
4 oz. apple cider vinegar
4 oz. chopped parsley

8 plain yoghourts
2 oz. Barbados sugar
sea salt
paprika

Make dressing of yoghourt, vinegar, sugar, salt and paprika. Slice cucumber finely and cover with dressing, sprinkle with parsley.

165. Russian Salad

5 lb. cooked peas
2 lb. diced carrots
2 lb. cooked diced potatoes
½ lb. diced cooked beetroot

sea salt
pepper
garlic salt
paprika
2 pints salad cream

Mix all the vegetables together in a big bowl, season well, and stir in the salad cream.

166. Chicory Salad

16 heads chicory
8 green peppers
8 oz. green olives

DRESSING
½ pint olive oil
juice of 8 lemons

2 oz. chopped mint
2 oz. French mustard
sea salt
garlic salt
pepper
1 oz. Barbados sugar

Wash and slice chicory heads, remove seeds and skin from inside peppers, slice finely, slice olives. Mix all ingredients together and stir in the dressing.

167. Banana and Walnut Salad

40 bananas	*1 lb. chopped walnuts*
juice of 8 lemons	*6 bundles watercress*
4 oz. chopped parsley	*½ pint salad cream*

Slice bananas into thin rounds, mix with lemon juice in bowl. Add chopped walnuts, salad cream and parsley. Decorate with watercress.

168. Celery Salad

16 heads celery	*½ pint salad cream*
4 oz. chopped parsley	

Wash and chop celery, mix with salad cream and sprinkle with parsley.

169. Celery and Egg Salad

16 heads celery	*2 chopped onions*
4 oz. chopped parsley	*2 oz. chopped walnuts*
16 hard-boiled eggs	*1 pint salad cream*

Wash and chop celery, mix with chopped hard-boiled eggs, parsley, nuts and onions. Stir in the salad cream.

SANDWICH FILLINGS

QUANTITIES TO MAKE 60 ROUNDS:
4 × 2-LB. WHOLEWHEAT LOAVES, 2 LB. BUTTER

170. Sardine and Tomato

4 × 8-oz. tins sardines	*4 lb. tomatoes*

Mash sardines with chopped tomatoes.

171. Liver Pâté and Cucumber

8 × 4-oz. tins liver pâté   4 thinly sliced cucumbers
or
2 lb. home-made liver pâté

Spread pâté on bread and cover with thin slices of cucumber.

172. Ham Eggs Chives

1½ lb. cooked ham   2 oz. chopped chives
18 hard-boiled eggs

Chop all ingredients, mix together with a little butter and spread on bread.

173. Honey and Nuts

1 lb. peanuts, walnuts or cashews
1 lb. Mexican honey

Chop or grate nuts very finely and mix with honey.

174. Marmite and Watercress

4 bundles watercress   4 oz. Marmite or Yeasty

Spread bread with yeast extract, chop watercress and sprinkle on top.

175. Bacon

1½ lb. streaky bacon

Grill bacon cut in small pieces and sprinkle on bread.

176. Cheese and Celery

12 oz. Cheddar or Gorganzola cheese
1 head celery

Grate cheese and chop up celery very finely, mix together with a little butter.

177. Curried Egg

18 hard-boiled eggs   *2 oz. curry powder*

Chop eggs finely, mix with a little butter and add the curry powder.

178. Banana and Walnut

12 bananas   *4 oz. walnuts*

Mash bananas lightly, chop the walnuts and mix together.

179. Cheese and Tomato

12 oz. Cheddar cheese   *2 lb. tomatoes*

Grate cheese, chop tomatoes and mix together.

180. Peanut Butter and Cucumber or Celery

1 lb. peanut butter   *4 thinly sliced cucumbers*
                                            or
                              1 head celery finely chopped

Spread bread with peanut butter and cover with cucumber or celery.

181. Dried Fruit and Nut

1 lb. raisins, dates or figs
8 oz. walnuts, cashews or peanuts

Mince fruit and nuts together and add a little water to make a paste.

182. Anchovy and Egg

18 hard-boiled eggs   *2 oz. anchovy essence*

Chop eggs with a little butter, add the anchovy essence.

183. Peanut Butter and Soya Flour

1 lb. peanut butter   *4 oz. salad cream*
4 oz. soya flour

Blend together.

*   *   *

HOMEMADE SALAD CREAM

4 egg yolks
4 dessertspoons apple cider vinegar
pinch of sea salt, pepper and Barbados sugar
1 pint vegetable oil

Beat up egg yolks, vinegar and seasonings, add the vegetable oil and continue beating until thick and creamy.

Chapter 8

HERBS AND SPICES

Allspice
Basil
Bay Leaves
Caraway Seed
Cayenne Pepper
Celery Salt
Chilli Powder
Chives
Cinnamon
Cloves
Cumin Seed
Curry Powder
Garlic Salt
Ginger
Marjoram
Mint
Mixed Spice
Nutmeg
Paprika
Parsley
Rosemary

Herbs and Spices

Sage
Tarragon
Thyme
Turmeric
Bouquet Garni

8

Herbs and Spices

Allspice

Spice, sweet and mild. Used whole in pickles, chutney and stews.

Basil

A mild, sweet and pungent herb. Used in all tomato dishes, with cold rice salads, in egg sandwiches and with liver and lamb.

Bay Leaves

Mild and distinctive herb. Used in soups, stews, marinades, in boiling ox tongue, soused herrings, meat and fish casseroles. Add to milk when heating for sweet and savoury white sauces.

Caraway Seeds

Pleasant, slightly sharp flavour. Used in rye bread, seed cake, veal dishes, cheese spreads and with pork and goose.

Cayenne Pepper

Hot pungent flavour. Used in devilled dishes, in fish cakes and cheese dishes.

Celery Salt

Celery flavoured salt. Used in soups, stews and casseroles.

Chilli Powder

Warm with slight bite. Used in egg dishes, with baked beans and in Mexican dishes.

Chives

A herb with delicate onion flavour. Used in salads, cheese dips, omelettes, with tomatoes and in soups.

Cinnamon

Sweet and spicy with a distinctive flavour. Used in buns, fruit cakes, ginger bread, milk puddings and apple pie.

Cloves

A strong spice. Used whole in apple pies and puddings, with baked ham, bread sauce and ground in fruit cakes, buns and mincemeat.

Cumin Seed

Similar to Caraway. Used in devilled dishes, in cheese dips, with minced beef, cabbage, sauerkraut and fish.

Curry Powder

Strong and spicy. Used in curries, sandwich fillings, stuffed eggs and savoury meat dishes.

Garlic Salt

Salt flavoured with garlic. May be used as a substitute for garlic and used for seasoning soup, stews etc.

Ginger

A hot rich spice. Used whole in pickles, chutney, ginger beer and wine. Ground in puddings, cakes, biscuits, gingerbread, treacle tart, curries and with melon and Chinese dishes.

Marjoram

A herb with a delicate, slightly bitter flavour. Used with lamb, beef, veal, pork and poultry, with omelettes, fish, soufflés, stews, vegetables and salads.

Mint

A herb with a fresh, piercing scent. Add to new potatoes, peas, mint sauce, cream cheese and sprinkle on tomatoes. Used in long refreshing drinks.

Mixed Spice

Aromatic blend of sweet spices. Used in cakes, biscuits, stewed fruit, and puddings.

Nutmeg

Sweet, exotic and spicy. Used in doughnuts, custards, junkets, and puddings. With ice cream, stewed fruit, spicy cakes and cheese sauce.

Paprika

Mild, slightly sweet-flavoured spice. Used in goulash, chicken in paprika sauce, egg and cheese dishes, canapés and rice dishes. Used also for colour as a garnish.

Herbs and Spices

Parsley

Herb with a mild, agreeable flavour and tremendous nutritional value. Used to sprinkle on soups, stews, on rice and tomatoes, salads, minced meat, in parsley sauce, rissoles, savoury meat roll. Used as a garnish on sandwiches, meat and fish dishes.

Rosemary

Distinctive, delicate and sweetish flavour. Sprinkled over lamb before roasting, added to stewing lamb and beef casseroles.

Sage

Strong, aromatic herb. Used with baked pork dishes and for poultry stuffings.

Tarragon

Fresh, pleasant-flavoured herb. Used with salads, chicken dishes, vinegar, fish and shell fish and in Hollandaise, Bearnaise and Tartare Sauces.

Thyme

Pungent and penetrating-flavoured herb. Used in meat dishes, soups, bread stuffing with lemon and in forcemeat, for salads and tomatoes.

Turmeric

Clean, mild-flavoured spice. Used in pickles, relishes, salad dressings and to colour rice and curries.

Bouquet Garni

Three sprigs parsley, one sprig thyme, and one bay leaf tied together in a piece of muslin.

Chapter 9

BREAD—SCONES—CAKES—BISCUITS

184. Wholewheat Bread
185. Wholewheat Scones
186. Wholewheat Fruit Scones
187. Wholewheat Drop Scones
188. Date and Walnut Loaf
189. Treacle Loaf
190. Allbran Loaf
191. Irish Tea Loaf
192. Nut and Raisin Bread
193. Farmhouse Fruit Bread
194. Nut and Honey Roll
195. Honey and Almond Cake
196. Rich Fruit Cake
197. Basic Sponge Cake
198. Pineapple Cake
199. Raspberry Cake
200. Orange Cake
201. Lemon Cake
202. Coffee Cake
203. Chocolate Cake
204. Walnut Cake
205. Cherry Cake
206. Ginger Cake

207. Choux Pastry
208. Éclairs
209. Cream Puffs
210. Meringues
211. Doughnuts
212. Hot Cross Buns
213. Date Crunchies
214. Flapjacks
215. Jumbles
216. Melting Moments
217. Carlisle Cookies
218. Ginger Crunchies
219. Shortbread
220. Coconut Biscuits
221. Chocolate Crunchies
222. Almond Slices
223. Japs
224. Nut Cookies
225. Coffee and Walnut Cookies
226. Coffee Sponge Fingers
227. Chocolate Fudge Fingers
228. Nutties
229. Macaroons
230. Cheese Biscuits
231. Cheese Straws
232. Cheeselets
233. Cheese Puffs
234. Baked Cheese Puffs
235. Curry Biscuits

9

Bread—Scones—Cakes—Biscuits

184. Wholewheat Bread

6 lb. plain wholewheat flour	*8 tbs. tepid water*
1 oz. dried yeast	*2 tbs. Barbados sugar*
2 tbs. salt	*3 pints tepid water*

Mix flour, sugar and salt. Cream yeast in 8 tablespoons tepid water, then dissolve in 3 pints tepid water. Add to flour, turn onto floured surface and knead well. Place dough in a bowl, cover with a damp cloth and leave for about an hour in a warm place to rise, turn out again on to floured surface and knead lightly. Divide into six pieces and place in greased tins, leave for another 40 minutes before baking in oven 400° F. or Reg. 6 for 45 minutes.

185. Wholewheat Scones

1½ lb. self-raising whole-wheat flour	*1½ tsps. sea salt*
	¼ pint milk
6 oz. margarine	*1 egg*

Rub margarine into salted flour, add milk to make soft dough, turn on to floured surface, roll lightly and quickly until dough is ¾ inch thick. Cut into rounds, brush with beaten egg and bake on greased tins in oven 450° F. or Reg. 8 for 15 minutes.

186. Wholewheat Fruit Scones

1½ lb. self-raising whole-wheat flour	¾ pint milk
6 oz. margarine	4 oz. Barbados sugar
1½ tsps. sea salt	8 oz. sultanas
	1 egg

Rub margarine into salted flour, add sugar and sultanas, add milk to make a soft dough, turn on to floured surface, roll lightly and quickly until dough is ¾ inch thick. Cut into rounds, brush with beaten egg and bake on greased tins in oven 450° F. or Reg. 8 for 15 minutes.

187. Wholewheat Drop Scones

1½ lb. self-raising whole-wheat flour	2 oz. Barbados sugar
	1½ pints milk
3 eggs	3 tsps. cream of tartar
1 tsp. salt	

Mix flour, salt, sugar, and cream of tartar in a basin, add eggs and milk to make a smooth thick batter, beat for 6 minutes. Drop mixture in tablespoons on to hot, greased griddle or heavy frying-pan, cook until pale brown on one side, turn and cook on other side, butter thickly.

188. Date and Walnut Loaf

3½ lb. self-raising whole-wheat flour	1 lb. Barbados sugar
1 tsp. salt	8 oz. margarine
2 lb. chopped dates	4 eggs
8 oz. chopped walnuts	3 pints boiling water

Mix all ingredients, add boiling water and beat well. Bake in greased tins in oven 400° F. or Reg. 6 for 1 hour.

189. Treacle Loaf

3 lb. self-raising whole-wheat flour	3 pints milk
3 tsps. salt	12 oz. Barbados sugar
6 tsps. mixed spice	12 tbs. black treacle
12 oz. butter	1½ lb. seeded raisins
	6 eggs

Put butter, milk, sugar, treacle and raisins into a saucepan and warm gently until the butter is melted, cool and add the beaten eggs. Mix flour, salt, and spice in a big basin, add milk mixture and stir well. Turn into greased loaf tins and bake for 45 minutes in oven 375° F. or Reg. 5.

190. Allbran Loaf

8 cups Allbran	8 eggs
8 cups Barbados sugar	8 cups wholewheat self-raising flour
8 cups sultanas	
8 cups milk	

Soak Allbran, sugar, sultanas and milk overnight. Next morning stir in the eggs and flour. Bake in oven 375° F. or Reg. 5 for 1 hour in well-greased tin.

191. Irish Tea Loaf

2 lb. currants	8 eggs
2 lb. sultanas	8 tbs. marmalade
2 lb. raisins	8 tbs. mixed spice
2 lb. Barbados sugar	4 lb. self-raising whole-wheat flour
4 cups cold tea	

Soak the mixed fruit and sugar in the tea overnight. Stir in the eggs, marmalade and spice with 3 tsps. of salt, add the flour and stir well. Pour into greased tins and bake in oven 400° F. or Reg. 6 for 1 hour.

192. Nut and Raisin Bread

3 lb. self-raising whole-
   wheat flour
1 tsp. salt
8 oz. margarine
8 oz. Barbados sugar

8 oz. raisins
1 lb. chopped nuts
4 eggs
2 pints milk

Rub margarine into salted flour, add dry ingredients and mix to a soft dough with egg and milk. Bake in oven 400° F. or Reg. 6 for 1 hour in well-greased tins.

193. Farmhouse Fruit Bread

6 oz. sultanas
6 oz. currants
6 oz. raisins
6 oz. dates

4 lb. self-raising whole-
   wheat flour
½ pint golden syrup
1 pint fresh tea

Melt the syrup in the hot tea, pour into flour and add the dried fruit, pour into well-greased tins and bake in oven 375° F. or Reg. 5 for 1½ hours. Slice when cool and spread with butter.

194. Nut and Honey Roll

2 lb. margarine
4 lb. plain wholewheat flour
2 tsps. salt
8 oz. Barbados sugar
8 eggs

juice of 4 lemons
2 lb. chopped walnuts
1 oz. candied peel
honey to coat the pastry

Rub the margarine into the salted flour and add the sugar, mix to a stiff paste with the eggs and lemon juice, if necessary add a little water. Roll out into an oblong shape and brush with honey, sprinkle with nuts and peel. Roll up like a swiss roll, sprinkle with Barbados sugar and bake on a greased tin in oven 450° F. or Reg. 8 for about 20 minutes.

195. Honey and Almond Cake

2 lb. margarine	TOPPING AND FILLING
1 lb. Barbados sugar	1½ lb. margarine or butter
1 lb. thick honey	½ lb. thick honey
3 lb. self-raising whole-wheat flour	1½ lb. Barbados sugar
16 eggs	12 oz. flaked almonds
½ pint milk	(toasted)

Cream butter, sugar and honey together, add eggs, flour and milk. Put in well-greased tins and bake in oven 375° F. or Reg. 5 for 45 minutes. Cream the filling together and put half in the middle of the cake and the other half all over the outside. Scatter with flaked almonds.

196. Rich Fruit Cake

3 lb. butter	1 lb. raisins
2 lb. Barbados sugar	1 lb. cherries
18 eggs	1 lb. almonds
3 lb. wholewheat flour	1 lb. candied peel
2 lb. currants	2 oz. mixed spice
2 lb. sultanas	

Cream butter and sugar, add eggs, then flour. Sprinkle in the rest of the ingredients, mix well, put in well-greased and papered tins and bake in oven 300° F. or Reg. 2 for 1 hour and a further 1½ hours at 250° F. or Reg ½.

197. Basic Sponge Cake

3 lb. margarine	½ cup hot water
1½ lb. Barbados sugar	18 eggs
3 lb. self-raising whole-wheat flour	

H

Cream margarine and sugar, add eggs then flour with $\frac{1}{2}$ cup hot water. Bake in greased tins in oven 400° F. or Reg. 6 for 30 minutes.

198. Pineapple Cake

Make basic sponge mixture recipe 197 adding 4 oz. pineapple pieces to mixture instead of hot water. Make butter icing with 1 lb. butter or margarine, 1 lb. Barbados sugar and 6 oz. pineapple juice. Sandwich cakes together with butter icing, spread over top and decorate with slices of pineapple.

199. Raspberry Cake

As recipe 198 using 2 lb. fresh raspberries instead of pineapple pieces. Flavour icing with juice from raspberries.

200. Orange Cake

As recipe 198 using fruit and juice of 6 oranges instead of pineapple.

201. Lemon Cake

Make as recipe 198 using fruit and juice of 6 lemons instead of pineapple.

202. Coffee Cake

Make as recipe 198 using $\frac{1}{2}$ cup hot coffee instead of water and flavouring butter icing with coffee. Decorate with walnuts.

203. Chocolate Cake

Make basic sponge mixture 197 but substituting $\frac{1}{2}$ lb. cocoa for $\frac{1}{2}$ lb. flour. Make butter icing as in recipe 198 using 4 oz. cocoa instead of pineapple. Decorate with glacé cherries.

204. Walnut Cake

Make basic sponge mixture recipe 197 adding 1 lb. walnuts chopped fairly small. Use unflavoured butter icing and decorate with walnuts.

205. Cherry Cake

Make basic sponge mixture recipe 197 adding 1½ lb. glacé cherries. Cook for 1½ hours in oven 400° F. or Reg. 6. Use plain butter icing and decorate with glacé cherries.

206. Ginger Cake

2 lb. margarine	*4 oz. ground ginger*
2 lb. Barbados sugar	*8 eggs*
2 lb. black treacle	*4 oz. powdered cinnamon*
2 lb. self-raising whole-wheat flour	*2 teacups hot milk*

Cream margarine and sugar, add treacle and eggs, then other dry ingredients, add hot milk and pour into well-greased shallow tins and bake in oven 350° F. or Reg. 4 for 2 hours.

207. Choux Pastry

½ lb. margarine	*16 eggs*
1 lb. wholewheat flour	*1 tsp. sea salt*
1 pint hot water	

Bring margarine, salt and water to the boil in a saucepan. Take pan off the heat and add the flour all at once, stirring quickly to a smooth paste. Return to heat for a few moments stirring all the time, then remove from heat once again and add the eggs one by one, beating well until they are all absorbed and the mixture smooth and light. Allow to cool before using.

208. Éclairs

Choux pastry (recipe 207 will make 6 dozen small éclairs)

ÉCLAIR TOPPING
8 oz. cocoa or 8 oz. cooking chocolate
1 lb. Barbados sugar
2 oz. water

Pipe choux pastry on to greased baking tins in long rolls, and bake in oven 375° F. or Reg. 5 for ½ hour. When cooked split each éclair down the side, scrape out the soft centre and fill with cream. Decorate tops with chocolate.

209. Cream Puffs

1 lb. choux pastry (recipe 207)

Drop spoonfuls of choux pastry on to greased and floured baking trays, cook in oven 450° F. or Reg. 8 for 40 minutes approx. They are cooked when there is no moisture on the outside and they are golden in colour. When puffs are cold make a hole in the bottom of each and fill with cream.

210. Meringues

18 egg whites   *2 lb. Demerara sugar*

Whip up egg whites in mixer, balloon whisk speed 3, gradually add the sugar and when stiff pipe on to well-oiled trays and bake in oven 250° F. or Reg. ½ for 2 or 3 hours until crisp and golden. Sandwich together with cream.

211. Doughnuts

3 lb. plain wholewheat flour	*1 pint warm milk*
1 tsp. salt	*6 eggs*
12 oz. margarine	*cinnamon flavoured*
6 oz. Barbados sugar	*Demerara sugar*
3 oz. yeast	*oil for deep frying*

Rub margarine into salted flour, add sugar. Cream yeast and eggs with warm milk and pour into flour mixture, mix well and put on one side to rise to double its size (approx. 1 hour). Knead lightly and roll out ½ inch thick, cut into rings, then cut out the centre of each and allow to prove on warm tray for 5 minutes. Deep fry and toss in cinnamon-flavoured Demerara sugar.

212. Hot Cross Buns

3 lb. plain wholewheat flour	*4 eggs*
1½ tsps. salt	*1½ pints warm milk*
6 oz. margarine	*6 oz. currants*
12 oz. Barbados sugar	*6 oz. peel*
3 tsps. mixed spice	*few strips pastry to make*
1½ oz. yeast	*crosses*

Rub margarine into salted flour, add sugar and spice. Cream yeast and eggs with warm milk, pour into flour mixture and leave on one side to rise to double its size (approx. 1 hour). When well risen knead lightly, working in the fruit, divide into 60 pieces, form into rounds, flatten slightly and allow to prove for 15 minutes. Put pastry crosses on top of each bun, brush with egg and bake in oven 450° F. or Reg. 8 for 20 minutes.

213. Date Crunchies

3 lb. oat flakes	2 lb. Barbados sugar
2½ lb. plain wholewheat flour	4 lb. dates
4 lb. margarine	1½ pints water

Rub fat into dry ingredients, spread layer of mixture on greased tin and spread with dates softened with a little water. Cover with another layer of mixture and bake in oven 375° F. or Reg. 5 for 40 minutes, cut into slices.

214. Flapjacks

2 lb. margarine	¾ pint golden syrup
1 lb. lard	4 lb. rolled oats
2 lb. Barbados sugar	

Melt fat, sugar, and syrup in a saucepan, add the oats, spread the mixture on to greased trays and bake in oven 400° F. or Reg. 5 for 20 minutes. Mark into portions whilst still warm.

215. Jumbles

1 lb. plain wholewheat flour	½ pint golden syrup
1 lb. Barbados sugar	4 tsps. ground ginger
1 lb. margarine	

Melt fat, syrup, and sugar in a saucepan, stir in the rest of the ingredients. Place the mixture in teaspoonfuls onto a greased tray fairly far apart, bake in oven 400° F. or Reg. 6 for a few minutes. When cooked, cool slightly, then with a knife lift them off the tray round the handle of a wooden spoon, slip off and follow quickly with the other ones. Should they harden too soon put the tray over the heat for a minute or two and carry on. Fill with whipped cream for parties.

216. Melting Moments

2 lb. margarine	4 eggs
1 lb. Barbados sugar	Cornflakes or Rice Crispies
2 lb. self-raising whole- wheat flour	(crushed)

Rub margarine into flour, add the sugar, then the eggs making a firm dough. Roll into small balls, cover with cornflakes or crispies, and bake on a greased tray in oven 400° F. or Reg. 6 for 15 minutes.

217. Carlisle Cookies

1 lb. margarine	FILLING
1 lb. Barbados sugar	1 lb. butter
1 tbs. golden syrup	1 lb. Barbados sugar
¾ lb. plain wholewheat flour	1 cup milk powder
12 oz. Cornflakes	1 cup cocoa
8 oz. Quick Quaker Oats	

Melt margarine, sugar, and syrup in a saucepan, add the oats, cornflakes and flour. Put in teaspoonfuls on to a greased tray and bake in oven 375° F. or Reg. 5 for 15 minutes approx. Sandwich together with chocolate butter filling.

218. Ginger Crunchies

2 lb. plain wholewheat flour	1 lb. margarine or butter
4 tsps. ground ginger	1 lb. Barbados sugar
4 eggs	preserved ginger
2 tbs. black treacle	

Rub the fat into the flour, then add the sugar and ground ginger, followed by the beaten eggs and treacle. Roll out the dough and cut into the required number of shapes, decorate with pre-served ginger and bake in oven 375° F. or Reg. 5 for 15 minutes.

219. Short Bread

2 lb. plain wholewheat flour   *8 oz. Demerara sugar*
1½ lb. butter

Rub fat into flour, add sugar, mix until firm dough is formed. Roll into a rectangle ½ inch thick, prick, and bake in oven 375° F. or Reg. 5 for 20 minutes, cut into fingers whilst still hot.

220. Coconut Biscuits

2 lb. margarine   *2 lb. Demerara sugar*
2 lb. plain wholewheat flour   *4 eggs*
2 lb. desiccated coconut

Mix dry ingredients to a paste with eggs and margarine, roll out thinly and cut into biscuit shapes. Bake in oven 375° F. or Reg. 5 for 15 minutes.

221. Chocolate Crunchies

1 lb. margarine   *1 lb. cooking chocolate*
12 oz. Barbados sugar   *1 lb. self-raising whole-*
4 eggs   *wheat flour*
4 tbs. milk   *12 oz. rolled oats*

Cream margarine and sugar, beat in the eggs then the milk and the chocolate cut into small pieces, finally the flour and the oats. Place portions of mixture 2 inches apart on greased trays and bake in oven 375° F. or Reg. 5 for 15 minutes.

222. Almond Slices

1½ lb. plain wholewheat flour   *8 oz. blanched and chopped*
1 lb. butter or margarine   *almonds*
1 lb. Barbados sugar   *milk to mix*
8 eggs

Cream butter and sugar together, add the beaten eggs and the flour, add sufficient milk to make a stiff batter. Pour into greased tins, sprinkle the top with chopped almonds and bake in oven 375° F. or Reg. 5 for 15 minutes. Cut into slices and leave until cold.

223. Japs

16 egg whites	BUTTER ICING
2 lb. Demerara sugar	*8 oz. butter*
2 lb. ground almonds	*8 oz. Barbados sugar*
a few drops of almond	*coffee essence*
essence	*½ cup milk powder*

Half whisk the egg whites, gradually sprinkle in the sugar and the ground almonds and beat until stiff. Spread mixture over oiled and floured tins and bake in oven 375° F. or Reg. 5 until almost set, then mark into rounds of 1½ inches with a cutter, return to the oven and cook until quite firm. Remove the rounds from the tin and put them on a wire rack to cool, continue to cook the trimmings until quite dry. When cold, crush the trimmings with a rolling pin and pass through a wire sieve. Put butter icing into a forcing bag with a plain pipe and put a blob of butter icing on to half of the biscuits, place the other halves on top and squeeze so that the icing comes out at the sides, spread round the sides with a small knife. Cover tops with butter icing and coat all over with the prepared crumbs. Decorate each biscuit with a chocolate drop.

224. Nut Cookies

1½ lb. margarine	*1½ lb. self-raising whole-*
1 lb. Barbados sugar	*wheat flour*
1 lb. chopped walnuts	*8 eggs*
	halved walnuts to decorate

Cream margarine and sugar, add nuts, eggs, and flour. Roll

into small balls, flatten slightly; put a walnut on each and bake in oven 400° F. or Reg. 6 for 15 minutes. These can be varied with addition of either 1 lb. desiccated coconut or 1 lb. cornflakes instead of 1 lb. of flour.

225. Coffee and Walnut Cookies

1½ lb. margarine	*8 tsps. coffee essence*
1½ lb. Barbados sugar	*1 lb. chopped walnuts*
8 eggs	*8 tsps. mixed spice*
1½ lb. plain wholewheat flour	

Cream margarine and sugar, beat in the eggs, coffee essence, and nuts, add the flour and spice making a soft dough. Roll into small rounds and bake on greased tins in oven 400° F. or Reg. 6 for 15 minutes.

226. Coffee Sponge Fingers

16 eggs	*1 lb. plain wholewheat flour*
2 tbs. Nescafé diluted in	*½ lb. blanched and chopped*
3 oz. hot water	*almonds*
1 lb. Barbados sugar	*2 lb. apricot jam or honey*

Beat eggs until light and frothy, beat in the coffee essence and the sugar; beat for 5 minutes and then lightly fold in the flour. Pour the mixture into flat tins lined with greased paper and bake in oven 375° F. or Reg. 5 for 15 minutes. Turn out onto flat tray, when cool spread top with honey or jam and sprinkle with chopped almonds. Cut into required number of slices.

227. Chocolate Fudge Fingers

1 lb. 12 oz. self-raising	*1½ lb. margarine*
wholewheat flour	*1½ lb. Barbados sugar*
4 oz. cocoa	*8 oz. chopped walnuts*
½ tsp. salt	*4 eggs*

Mix flour, cocoa, salt, cut in the margarine, add sugar and nuts. Stir in the beaten eggs. Spread in greased tins and bake in oven 375° F. or Reg. 5 for 40 minutes, cut into fingers and cool.

228. Nutties

1 lb. self-raising whole-wheat flour	*½ tsp. salt*
	8 oz. chopped walnuts
1 lb. butter or margarine	*8 oz. chopped hazelnuts*
1 lb. Barbados sugar	*warm milk to mix*

Rub the butter into the flour, sugar, salt and nuts, mix to a stiff dough with warm milk, form into little balls, stick a chopped nut on top and bake in oven 400° F. or Reg. 6 for 15 minutes.

229. Macaroons

2 lb. ground almonds	*16 egg whites*
2 lb. Demerara sugar	*blanched almonds to*
20 drops almond essence	*decorate*

Mix together almonds, sugar, and essence. Lightly beat egg whites and slowly add to almond mixture to form fairly stiff dough. Divide into small balls and place an almond on each. Bake on greased trays in oven 350° F. or Reg. 4 for 15 minutes.

230. Cheese Biscuits

12 oz. butter or margarine	*cayenne pepper*
1 lb. plain wholewheat flour	*8 egg yolks*
1 lb. dry grated cheese	*4 tsps. Worcester sauce*
1 tsp. salt	

Rub fat into salted flour, add cheese and a pinch of cayenne pepper, mix to a paste with egg yolks and Worcester sauce.

Roll out thinly and bake in oven 250 ° F. or Reg. ½ until golden brown.

231. Cheese Straws

12 oz. plain wholewheat
  flour
8 oz. butter or margarine
8 oz. Parmesan cheese or
  dry Cheddar

1 tsp. salt and 1 tsp.
  cayenne pepper
4 egg yolks

Rub fat into seasoned flour, add cheese and mix to a smooth paste with egg yolks and a little water. Roll out pastry and cut into strips, bake in oven 375° F. or Reg. 5 for 15 minutes.

232. Cheeselets

3 lb. plain wholewheat flour
16 tsps. Marmite
1½ lb. margarine

2 lb. grated Cheddar
salt and pepper
water to mix
1 egg

Rub fat into seasoned flour, add cheese. Dissolve Marmite in a little cold water and sprinkle into flour mixture, knead to make a stiff dough. Roll out to approximately ¼ inch thickness, cut into small shapes, place on baking tray and brush with Marmite and beaten egg. Bake in oven 375° F. or Reg. 5 for 15 minutes.

233. Cheese Puffs

1 lb. grated cheese
1 lb. plain wholewheat flour
8 eggs

salt and pepper
cayenne pepper
deep fat for frying

Mix cheese and flour, add egg yolks and seasonings. Whip egg whites and fold into mixture. Drop teaspoonfuls of the mixture into hot fat and fry until golden brown, drain on greaseproof paper.

234. Baked Cheese Puffs

2 lb. choux pastry (recipe 207)
8 egg yolks
little milk
1½ lb. grated cheese

Make 2 lb. choux pastry, put teaspoonfuls of the mixture on greased and floured baking trays, brush over tops with egg yolk diluted with a little milk and sprinkle with cheese. Bake in oven 375° F. or Reg. 5 for 30–40 minutes. Serve piping hot.

235. Curry Biscuits

1 lb. plain wholewheat flour
4 tsps. curry powder
salt and pepper
1 lb. grated cheese
1½ lb. margarine
8 egg yolks

Mix flour, curry powder, salt, pepper, and cheese together and rub in the fat. Mix to a stiff dough with egg yolks and roll out, stamp into small biscuits with a cutter and bake in oven 375° F. or Reg. 5 for 15 minutes.

MENUS

MENU 1st WEEK

	Breakfast	Lunch	Supper
Monday	Muesli Scrambled Eggs on Toast Honey—Toast	Grilled Lamb Chops Cauliflower Mashed Potatoes Pineapple Upside- Down Cake Custard	Soup Macaroni Cheese Raw Vegetable Salad Fruit—Peanut Butter
Tuesday	Porridge Bacon and Tomatoes Honey—Toast	Roast Beef Yorkshire Pudding Roast Potatoes Swedes Pears and Semolina	Soup Quiche Lorraine Cheese Fruit
Wednesday	Cornflakes Chipolata Sausages Honey—Toast	Kedgeree Carrots Mashed Potatoes Baked Apples Custard	Grapefruit Hamburgers Sliced Tomatoes Cheese Jam

Day			
Thursday	Muesli Kippers Honey—Toast	Chicken and Mushroom Pie Mashed Potatoes Peas Fruit Salad	Soup Fried Egg on Baked Beans Raw Vegetable Salad Cheese Fruit
Friday	Porridge Egg and Bacon Honey—Toast	Curry and Rice Sliced Tomatoes and Cucumbers Mashed Potatoes Pineapple Meringue	Soup Welsh Rarebit Celery Cheese Fruit
Saturday	Oat Crunchies Mushrooms on Fried Bread Honey—Toast	Sausages Mashed Potatoes Cabbage Banana Custard	Soup Fried Rice Cheese Fruit
Sunday	Muesli Boiled Eggs Honey—Toast	Sweet and Sour Pork Fried Rice Brussels Sprouts Trifle	Soup Sardine Salad Cheese Fruit

MENU 2ND WEEK

	Breakfast	Lunch	Supper
Monday	Porridge Fish Fingers Honey—Toast	Stewed Steak Braised Celery Boiled Potatoes Cherry Tartlets	Soup Hot Dogs Raw Vegetable Salad Cheese Fruit
Tuesday	Cornflakes Egg Fritters Honey—Toast	Liver and Bacon Mashed Potatoes Cabbage Apple Crunch Custard	Soup Minced Chicken on Toast Cheese Fruit
Wednesday	Muesli Bacon and Beans Honey—Toast	Roast Pork Apple Sauce Roast Potatoes Brussels Sprouts Chocolate Mousse	Melon Curried Eggs and Rice Tomatoes Cheese Marmite

	Breakfast	Lunch	Supper
Thursday	Porridge Scrambled Eggs on Toast Honey—Toast	Irish Stew Boiled Potatoes Peas Pineapple Fritters	Soup Cauliflower Cheese Baked Potatoes Fruit Nuts
Friday	Oat Crunchies Chipolata Sausages Honey—Toast	Savoury Meat Roll Mashed Potatoes Carrots Fruit Jelly	Soup Spaghetti Bolognaise Raw Vegetable Salad Cheese Fruit
Saturday	Muesli Egg and Bacon Honey—Toast	Minced Beef Mashed Potatoes Cauliflower Apricot Sponge Custard	Soup Spam Fritters Baked Beans Tomatoes Cheese Fruit
Sunday	Cornflakes Tomatoes on Fried Bread Honey—Toast	Boiled Beef Dumplings Carrots Onions Cabbage Lemon Meringue Pie	Soup Sausage Rolls Tomatoes Cheese Fruit

MENU 3RD WEEK

	Breakfast	Lunch	Supper
Monday	Porridge Boiled Eggs Honey—Toast	Steak and Kidney Pie Mashed Potatoes Swedes White Blancmange Jam	Soup Baked Lasagne Fruit Peanut Butter
Tuesday	Oat Crunchies Bacon and Mushrooms Honey—Toast	Roast Lamb Mint Sauce Roast Potatoes Leeks Apple Pie Custard	Soup Savoury Pancakes Cheese Fruit
Wednesday	Muesli Scrambled Eggs on Toast Honey—Toast	Chicken Fricassée Rice Mashed Potatoes Carrots Raspberry Mousse	Grapefruit Sausage Casserole Cheese Marmite

Day			
Thursday	Porridge Tomatoes on Fried Bread Honey—Toast	Braised Steak Boiled Potatoes Brussels Sprouts Sponge and Treacle	Soup Minced Ham on Toast Raw Vegetable Salad Cheese Fruit
Friday	Cornflakes Egg and Bacon Honey—Toast	Fried Fish Mashed Potatoes Cauliflower Mince Pies Custard	Soup Spam and Salad Baked Potatoes Cheese Fruit
Saturday	Porridge Chipolata Sausages Honey—Toast	Cottage Pie Mashed Potatoes Cabbage Creamed Rice and Prunes	Soup Mushroom Patties Sliced Tomatoes Cheese Fruit
Sunday	Muesli Fish Cakes Honey—Toast	Toad in the Hole Mashed Potatoes Beetroot Fruit Salad	Soup Poached Egg on Mashed Potatoes Cheese Sauce Raw Vegetable Salad Fruit Nuts

LIST OF WHOLEFOOD SUPPLIERS

The Brewhurst Trading Company, Oyster Lane, Byfleet,
Surrey
(Alfonal Group wholesale distributor of wholefoods to institutions and shops.)

Alfonal Ltd., Oyster Lane, Byfleet, Surrey

The Wholesale Health Service Ltd., Davis Road, Chessington,
Surrey
(Wholesale distributor of comprehensive range of wholefoods to shops and institutions.)

Cranks Ltd., William Blake House, Marshall Street, London,
W.1.
(Supplies bulk packs of a number of wholefoods suitable for small institutions or large families. List on request.)

Allisons Ltd., 210–214 Cambridge Heath Road, London, E.2.

Health Food Supply Co. Ltd., Holly Bank Mill, Bolton Street,
Radcliffe, Manchester

Lusty's Natural Products Ltd., Westcliffe-on-Sea, Essex

Granose Foods Ltd., Stanborough Park, Watford, Herts.

Dietmart Ltd., Woodlands Farm, Faygate, Sussex

Mapleton's Food Ltd., Moss Street, Garston, Liverpool

G. R. Lane, Health Products Ltd., Gloucester

Chiltern Herb Farms, Buckland Common, Tring, Herts.

W. Prewett Ltd., Stone Flour Mills, Horsham, Sussex

List of Wholefood Suppliers

The Wholefood Finder, Henry Doubleday Research Association, Bocking, Braintree, Essex
and
The Soil Association, New Bells Farm, Haughley, Stowmarket, Suffolk

(Magazine giving list of farms supplying free range eggs and compost-grown fruit and vegetables. It also lists the shops supplying, and in some cases delivering, wholefoods. It describes the nature of wholefoods and contains other interesting facts.)

INDEX

Allbran Loaf, 111
Allspice, 103
Almond Slices, 120
Almond Tart, 61
Anchovy and Egg Sandwich Filling, 100
Apple Crunch, 56
Apple Fritters, 53
Apple Meringue, 57
Apple Pie, 54
Apple Sauce, 27
Apple Sponge, 57
Apple Tart, 54
Apricot Crunch, 56
Apricot Flan, 58
Apricot Meringue, 57
Apricot Pie, 54
Apricot Sponge, 57
Apricot Tart, 55

Bacon and Baked Beans, 20
Bacon—Beans—Sauté Potatoes, 76
Bacon and Chipolata, 20
Bacon and Egg, 19
Bacon and Mushrooms, 20
Bacon Sandwich Filling, 98
Bacon and Sliced Tomatoes, 20
Baked Apples, 58
Baked Cheese Puffs, 125
Baked Cod Fillets, 39
Baked Lasagne, 82
Banana Custard, 59
Banana Fritters, 53
Banana and Walnut Salad, 97
Banana and Walnut Sandwich Filling, 99
Basic Sponge Cake, 113
Basil, 103

Bay Leaves, 103
Beetroot, 45
Beetroot Salad, 95
Blackberry and Apple Tart, 55
Boiled Bacon, 28
Boiled Beef, 27
Boiled Eggs, 22
Bouquet Garni, 106
Braised Steak, 27
Bread Sauce, 33
Broad Beans, 45
Brussels Sprouts, 45

Caraway Seed, 103
Carrots, 46
Carlisle Cookies, 119
Cauliflower, 46
Cauliflower Cheese, 73
Cauliflower Salad, 94
Cayenne Pepper, 103
Celery, 46
Celery and Egg Salad, 97
Celery Salad, 97
Celery Salt, 103
Cheese Biscuits, 123
Cheese and Celery Sandwich Filling, 99
Cheese Pudding, 74
Cheeselets, 124
Cheese Puffs, 124
Cheese Straws, 124
Cheese and Tomato Sandwich Filling, 99
Cherry Cake, 115
Cherry Flan, 59
Cherry Tartlets, 60
Chestnut and Sausage Meat Stuffing, 37

Index

Chicken Fricassée and Rice, 32
Chicken and Mushroom Pie, 32
Chicken Slaw, 36
Chicory Salad, 96
Chilli Powder, 104
Chipolata Sausages, 21
Chives, 104
Chocolate Blancmange, 66
Chocolate Cake, 114
Chocolate Crunchies, 120
Chocolate Fudge Fingers, 122
Chocolate Mousse, 67
Chocolate Tart, 61
Chocolate Sponge and Sauce, 66
Choux Pastry, 115
Cinnamon, 104
Cloves, 104
Coconut Biscuits, 120
Coffee Cake, 114
Coffee Mousse, 67
Coffee Sponge Fingers, 122
Coffee and Walnut Cookies, 122
Cold Meat and Salad, 83
Cold Ham—Corned Beef—Luncheon Meat, 36
Cottage Pie, 34
Cream of Celery Soup, 89
Cream of Chicken Soup, 89
Cream of Mushroom Soup, 89
Cream Puffs, 116
Cucumbers, 49
Cucumber Salad, 96
Cumin Seed, 104
Curry Biscuits, 125
Curried Eggs and Rice, 76
Curried Egg Sandwich Filling, 99
Curry Powder, 104
Curry and Rice, 29
Custard Tart, 60

Date Crunchies, 118
Date and Walnut Loaf, 110
Devilled Turkey, 38
Dried Fruit and Nut Sandwich Filling, 100
Doughnuts, 117
Dumplings, 27
Dutch Cabbage, 45

Éclairs, 116
Egg Fritters, 22
Egg Mayonnaise, 78
Egg Sauce, 40

Farmhouse Fruit Bread, 112
Fish Cakes, 22
Fish and Bacon Pie, 41
Fish Fingers, 21
Fish Pie, 40
Fish Slaw, 41
Flapjacks, 118
Fried Egg and Baked Beans, 75
Fried Cod Fillets, 39
Fried Rice, 80
Fruit Bread, 112
Fruit Flan, 59
Fruit Jelly, 68
Fruit Salad, 68

Garlic Salt, 104
Ginger, 105
Ginger Cake, 115
Ginger Crunchies, 119
Gooseberry Crunch, 56
Gooseberry Pie, 54
Gooseberry Tart, 55
Green Cabbage, 46
Green Salad, 95
Grilled Lamb Chops, 30
Grilled Pork Chops, 30

Hamburgers, 83
Ham, Egg and Chives Sandwich Filling, 98
Herrings, 77
Herring Roes on Toast, 78
Hollandaise Sauce, 39
Honey and Almond Cake, 113
Honey and Nut Sandwich Filling, 98
Horseradish Sauce, 25
Hot Cross Buns, 117
Hot Dogs, 84

Irish Stew, 30
Irish Tea Loaf, 111

Jam Tart, 61

Index

Japs, 121
Jumbles, 118

Kedgeree, 40
Kippers, 21

Leeks, 47
Lemon Cake, 114
Lemon Meringue Pie, 63
Lemon Mousse, 68
Lentil Soup, 90
Lettuce, 49
Lettuce Salad, 94
Liver and Bacon, 30
Liver Pâté and Cucumber Sandwich
    Filling, 98
Luncheon Meat, 36

Macaroons, 123
Marjoram, 105
Manchester Tart, 59
Marmite and Watercress Sandwich
    Filling, 98
Marmalade Tart, 62
Marrow, 47
Meat Cooking Times, 14
Meat Fritters, 83
Meat Loaf, 35
Melting Moments, 119
Meringues, 116
Metric Weights and Measures, 11
Minced Beef, 34
Minced Chicken on Toast, 79
Minced Ham on Toast, 79
Mince Pies, 62
Mint, 105
Mint Sauce, 26
Mixed Spice, 105
Muesli, 19
Mushroom Patties, 77
Mushrooms on Toast, 78

Nut Cookies, 121
Nutmeg, 105
Nutties, 123
Nut and Honey Roll, 112
Nut and Raisin Bread, 112

Onions, 47
Onion Sauce, 26
Orange Cake, 114
Oven Temperatures, 15
Oxtail Soup, 87

Pancakes, 64
Paprika, 105
Parsley, 106
Parsley Sauce, 28
Parsnips, 48
Peanut Butter and Cucumber or
    Celery Sandwich Filling, 99
Peanut Butter and Soya Flour Sand-
    wich Filling, 100
Pea Soup, 88
Pears and Rice, 64
Peas, 47
Peppers, 49
Pineapple Cake, 114
Pineapple Crunch, 56
Pineapple Fritters, 53
Pineapple Meringue, 58
Pineapple Upside-Down Cake, 63
Plum Crunch, 56
Poached Eggs on Mashed Potatoes
    with Cheese Sauce, 74
Porridge, 19
Potato Cakes and Bacon, 75
Potato Cheese and Bacon Pie, 74
Potato Salad, 93
Potato Soup, 88
Potatoes, 48
Prunes and Rice, 64

Queen's Pudding, 65
Quiche Lorraine, 81

Radishes, 49
Raspberry Cake, 114
Raspberry Mousse, 67
Raw Vegetable Salad, 93
Red Cabbage, 46
Rhubarb Crunch, 56
Rhubarb Tart, 55
Rice Pudding, 64
Rich Fruit Cake, 113
Rissoles, 36

Index

Roast Beef, 25
Roast Chicken, 33
Roast Lamb, 26
Roast Pork, 26
Roast Turkey, 37
Rosemary, 106
Runner Beans, 47
Russian Salad, 96

Sage, 106
Salad Cream, 100
Salade Niçoise, 95
Sardine Salad, 78
Sardine and Tomato Salad, 97
Sausages on Spaghetti, 79
Sausage Casserole, 82
Sausage Rolls, 81
Sausages, 34
Savoury Meat Roll, 29
Savoury Meat Balls, 80
Savoury Stuffing, 33
Savoury Pancakes, 83
Scotch Broth, 87
Scotch Eggs, 77
Scotch Woodcock, 76
Scrambled Eggs on Toast, 21
Semolina, 69
Shortbread, 120
Soya Beans, 49
Spaghetti Bolognaise, 80
Spaghetti Cheese, 73
Spanish Salad, 93
Spinach, 48
Sponge and Treacle, 65
Steak and Kidney Pie, 31
Steamed Sponge Pudding, 68
Steamed Fruit Sponge, 69

Steamed Ginger Pudding, 69
Stewed Apples, 58
Stewed Steak, 28
Stock, 90
Swedes, 48
Sweet and Sour Pork, 38

Tarragon, 106
Thyme, 106
Toad in the Hole, 35
Tomatoes, 49
Tomatoes on Fried Wholewheat Bread, 21
Tomato Salad, 94
Tomato Soup, 90
Treacle Loaf, 111
Treacle Tart, 62
Trifle, 65
Tuna Fish Salad, 41
Turmeric, 106
Turnips, 48

Veal and Ham Pie, 31
Vegetable Soup, 88

Walnut Cake, 115
Watercress, 49
Weights and Measures, 11
Welsh Rarebit, 75
White Blancmange and Jam, 67
Wholewheat Bread, 109
Wholewheat Breadcrumbs, 12
Wholewheat Drop Scones, 110
Wholewheat Fruit Scones, 110
Wholewheat Scones, 109

Yoghourt, 13